Vital Business

The Campaign for Social Science was launched in 2011 to promote social science to the UK Government and the wider public.

We campaign for policies that support social science inquiry in the UK, such as the retention of large-scale longitudinal research programmes. We promote social science on social media and at events.

The Campaign is supported by a coalition of universities, learned societies, charities and publishers.

To contact the Campaign, please call: +44 (0) 300 3933513 or email: campaign@acss.org.uk

For further information on the Campaign, see:

www.campaignforsocialscience.org.uk

Twitter: @CfSocialScience

Facebook: www.facebook.com/CfSocialScience

The Campaign is part of the Academy of Social Sciences, a company registered in England, number 3847936, and a registered charity, number 1088537.

Vital Business

THE ESSENTIAL ROLE OF THE SOCIAL SCIENCES IN THE UK PRIVATE SECTOR

Dr Ashley Lenihan
Senior Policy Advisor
Campaign for Social Science

Sharon Witherspoon
Head of Policy
Campaign for Social Science

with
Rory Alexander

ACADEMY *of* SOCIAL SCIENCES | CAMPAIGN *for* SOCIAL SCIENCE

Los Angeles I London I New Delhi
Singapore I Washington DC I Melbourne

ACADEMY
of SOCIAL SCIENCES | **CAMPAIGN** *for* SOCIAL SCIENCE

Academy of Social Science
c/o Knox Cropper LLP
5 Floor
65 Leadenhall Street
London
EC2A 3AD
Tel: 0300 3933513

⑤SAGE

Los Angeles | London | New Delhi
Singapore | Washington DC | Melbourne

SAGE Publications Ltd
1 Oliver's Yard
55 City Road
London EC1Y 1SP

SAGE Publications Inc.
2455 Teller Road
Thousand Oaks, California 91320

SAGE Publications India Pvt Ltd
B 1/I 1 Mohan Cooperative Industrial Area
Mathura Road
New Delhi 110 044

SAGE Publications Asia-Pacific Pte Ltd
3 Church Street
#10-04 Samsung Hub
Singapore 049483

Typeset by: C&M Digitals (P) Ltd, Chennai, India
Printed in the UK

British Library Cataloguing in Publication data

A catalogue record for this book is available from the
British Library

ISBN 978-1-5297-5416-2 (pbk)
ISBN: 978-1-5297-5419-3 (web PDF)

At SAGE we take sustainability seriously. Most of our products are printed in the UK using responsibly sourced
papers and boards. When we print overseas we ensure sustainable papers are used as measured by the PREPS
grading system. We undertake an annual audit to monitor our sustainability.

Contents

VITAL BUSINESS: the essential role of the social sciences in the UK private sector

Introduction

This report shows how social science knowledge and skills are used by, and are essential to, a number of UK private sector businesses. It is drawn from a small number of case studies that cover a range of sectors and types of work, from large multinationals to smaller firms, from manufacturing and retail to digital and other services to extractive industry. It is not a statistical analysis, though we know from many statistical sources (including our _**Positive Prospects**_ report) that social science graduates are found across all sectors in the UK, and their earnings are virtually as high as (or, for some social disciplines, higher than) graduates from so-called STEM (science, technology, engineering and mathematics) disciplines.[1]

But this report does not study individuals and their careers or earnings. It focuses instead on how a number of different UK private sector businesses actually use social science knowledge and skills (and employ social science graduates) to run and grow their firms. Though we use a case study approach here, we deliberately included a broad and diverse range of enterprises, including some that may be thought of mainly as 'STEM' enterprises. Because so many common themes occurred in the course of our interviews, we believe some general conclusions can be drawn to inform public policy and wider public discussion, as well as students making subject choices. In this introduction, we set out some of the conclusions, and look at what they may mean for policy and education in the UK.

General findings

- UK businesses across all sectors draw heavily on social science knowledge and skills.

  - In all cases, companies use social science knowledge and skills **to run their business** day to day. Economics, finance, accounting, management, law and human resources – all involving social science knowledge and skills, and trained social scientist employees – are deployed as part of ordinary management and governance.

  - For almost all companies, social science knowledge and skills are especially important for **leadership cadres**. Most of the people we spoke to pointed out (with no prompting) that leadership requires not only intuitive skills in managing people but some sort of training or qualification in management or economics to lead people and complex organisations. This mirrors the finding by the British Council, quoted in *Positive Prospects*, that leaders in the public sector often require (and are trained in) these skills too.

  - Most companies use social science knowledge and skills from a variety of disciplines **to understand and engage with their markets, clients and consumers**. They deploy knowledge and skills from economics, market research, psychology, political science and geography regularly, and are concerned to understand the current and future behaviours of their consumers, and the constraints and opportunities of the market structures in which they operate, including their geo-spatial and socio-economic characteristics.

  - Many companies use social science knowledge and skills **to analyse and manage risk and long-term strategies**. Often, this involves analysing the structures of risk and uncertainty in a particular market or social context, for example with political, economic, trade, investment, financial, regulatory, legal, environmental and strategic risk. Disciplinary knowledge and skills from economics, finance, political science, development studies, law, and geography are especially important here. In some cases, it also involves analysing risks associated with changes to individual behaviours, sometimes in very formal ways, in which case knowledge from psychology and behavioural economics also come into play. In other cases, scenario planning was central in considering how changes in social, political or economic factors could affect business.

  - Many companies use social science knowledge and skills **to develop new products or new ways of working**. While this is more obvious in some cases than in others, this frequently happens in multidisciplinary teams, often involving STEM sciences, or digital sciences working with social sciences to model how new products might be received, used, developed, or made more profitable. It also sometimes involves understanding the social and ethical impacts of a company's actions or products, or whether certain products or policies will be considered socially acceptable or desirable by consumers.

- ○ Some companies use social science knowledge and skills **in their Research and Development (R&D) for the longer term**. This is not just about investment in human capital and skills, but in innovations that lead to new services or products. We believe that much of this activity is not well captured by current rules (the so-called **'Frascati' rules for measuring R&D**), and are likely to be particularly important in the UK, where the service sector accounts for 80% of the economy. A wider definition (focusing less on publications or patents, as recommended by the House of Commons Science and Technology Committee Report on **'Balance and Effectiveness in Research and Innovation Spending'**),[2] could result not only in better measurement of it (and hence of the contribution of the social sciences) but better incentives for R&D too.

- Though we focus on concrete and specific examples of how UK businesses use knowledge or skills derived from the social sciences, we found that other skills also matter.

  - ○ We have welcomed the wider debate about the importance of **wider 'softer' skills** that social science graduates may have. Many of those we interviewed note these as well, mentioning curiosity, understanding people and their ranges of behaviours, and the ability to bring together evidence from disparate sources and present a clear narrative based on analysis that could inform and transform policies and actions within the company. But substantive social science knowledge and social science skills matter too.

- **Looking to the future – and most of those we spoke to take a long view – social science knowledge and skills are considered essential.**

  - ○ Most companies that we spoke to predict that more and deeper **cross-disciplinary working** will be needed in the future. This usually includes the need for traditional 'science' (STEM) disciplines to work in teams with social scientists who can understand the science substance but also bring knowledge about regulation, social and geo-spatial networks, and human behaviour together at various stages to inform strategies and product development. This was true in digital products or other services, and in industrial companies. Additionally, when companies consider the effect that artificial intelligence or digital developments might have on their business, or on broader society, they also tend to note the importance of the social sciences. This often goes beyond risk or reputation management, or consideration of regulatory regimes, and into social demand, and social responsibility, for the work of the company across the piece, and how they would work in a digital future. Taking the long view about geopolitical, environmental or technological risk, including how to respond to climate change, is almost always seen to have a strong social science dimension.

- In many of the companies we spoke to, firms draw not only on their own employees but also hire outside experts – from universities or consultancies – to tackle particular social science issues.

  o Again, these often involve multidisciplinary issues, spanning STEM and non-STEM subjects, including environmental issues or technological changes. Companies value having access to a developed system of outside experts, and in our interviews they noted the UK's excellence in having a strong university-based sector with experts who had diverse skills and knowledge on a range of topics.

Implications

Given the varied natures of the businesses we included, it was striking that so many of the same themes came up. The implications of these themes seem clear.

- It is unhelpful to posit a simple STEM/non-STEM divide in the usefulness of knowledge and skills in the private sector. We have already shown this is true of earnings and employment, where social science disciplines as a group fare about as well as graduates from STEM disciplines.[3] All the firms we spoke to value workforce diversity, not just in the traditional sense, but also in terms of their employees' experiential and disciplinary backgrounds, and their varied skills.

- Depth of knowledge and skills across a range of disciplines is needed and valued. Across the piece, the companies we spoke to value the right tool for the problem at hand, and view knowledge and skills as part of a system; they did not just focus on a few talented individuals. We believe this appreciation of science and social science as a system should be carried through to universities and areas of public policy (as we have advocated in our work on government funding for research and immigration regimes[4]). The acquisition of substantive knowledge and research skills through research-informed teaching is likely to be an important ingredient.

- Number and data skills are increasingly valued across all disciplines. This is true even of areas like HR (human resources) management, but is seen to be increasingly important within social science disciplines. Having these skills enriches understanding of individual, social, economic, and geo-spatial behaviours, and is crucial for understanding markets and many types of risk.

- Social science suffers from a 'brand' problem. It was striking that in some cases our initial approaches to the companies we spoke to led them to ask what the social sciences are. Some thought that 'social science' does not include anything involving number and data skills (so called 'quantitative' skills), and some even thought that economics is not a social science because it is largely a quantitative discipline. Make no mistake, these businesses also value case study and other 'qualitative' skills, and regularly use information other than large datasets to develop and grow their firms. But while the term 'STEM' now has widespread currency, and people understand what the 'arts and humanities' are – often linking them to the arts and creative sector in the UK – they often do not have an explicit understanding of what 'social science' is. Just as Molière's Monsieur Jordain has been speaking prose all his life without knowing it, the companies we interviewed use social science so deeply in so many facets of their work that some do not view it (with all its variation) as 'social science'. In many ways this may not matter, but it does when public policy often seems to value only STEM subjects, or the arts and creative sector of the economy. Whatever labels they employ, these businesses use, depend upon, and value social science knowledge and skills. That is surely the most important conclusion for public policy-makers and prospective students to draw from this report.

ATL

SFW

Notes

1   See A. Lenihan and S. Witherspoon (2018) Positive Prospects: Careers for social science graduates and why number and data skills matter. London: Campaign for Social Science/ Sage. https://campaignforsocialscience.org.uk/publications/positiveprospects/.

2   House of Commons Science and Technology Committee (2019) Balance and effectiveness in research and innovation spending. https://publications.parliament.uk/pa/cm201719/cmselect/cmsctech/1453/1453.pdf.

3   See Lenihan and Witherspoon, Positive Prospects; J. Britton, L. Dearden, L. van der Erve and B. Waltmann (2020) The impact of undergraduate degrees on lifetime earnings. Institute for Fiscal Studies. https://www.ifs.org.uk/publications/14729.

4   See, e.g., https://campaignforsocialscience.org.uk/wp-content/uploads/2019/10/An-Immigration-System-Fit-for-the-Science-System_.pdf; https://campaignforsocialscience.org.uk/wp-content/uploads/2019/06/The-Importance-of-the-Social-Sciences-for-the-Industrial-Strategy.pdf; https://campaignforsocialscience.org.uk/wp-content/uploads/2018/12/AcSS-and-CfSS-response-to-the-EU-Home-Affairs-Sub-Committee-Web-version.pdf.

About the case studies

Our main aim was to understand how UK private sector businesses use and value social science knowledge and skills. We approached a number of companies chosen deliberately from a wide range of sectors, including: manufacturing and retail; energy; market research; IT and digital services; transport and logistics; landscape architecture and planning; accounting and finance; and insurance. Virtually every firm we approached was willing to help.

In each case study, we start with a brief profile of the company and then report examples of how social science knowledge and skills are used. In addition to using publicly available documentation (such as company reports), we interviewed anywhere from one to six appropriate senior directors with an understanding of the business as a whole. While we started with the same basic questions in each case, much of each interview was 'unprompted' – we asked about general topics and then followed up on what interviewees told us with more specific questions. But we started with *their* descriptions.

For example, we asked each interviewee how their business used social scientists, or evidence from the social sciences. Many said that they do so to better understand their customer base or improve their strategy. What this means for each company, however, differed. For some, it means assessing the demographics of markets and consumer behaviour; analysing big data or conducting social surveys to better understand social and consumer trends; or seeking insights into the cultures and communities in which they operate. For others it means using econometric modelling to forecast economic, environmental, regulatory, and political risk to understand the future scenarios their businesses may need to plan for. For many, it means using basic research from social science disciplines to understand their own organisational psychology and improve business culture and employee well-being, as well as their 'bottom line'.

What do we mean when we say the 'social sciences'?

Whether or not companies used the term 'social sciences' when we first spoke with them, it was important that we had a clear definition. As in all the work of the **Academy of Social Sciences** and its **Campaign for Social Science**, we use a wide definition to reflect its diversity. In our classification, the social sciences encompass disciplines that apply social understanding in a systematic way to understand and solve problems in the world around us. These include disciplines that the Higher Education Statistics Agency counts as '*social studies*' (including economics, politics, sociology, social policy, social work, anthropology, human & social geography, and development studies); *business & administrative studies* (including business studies, management studies, finance, accounting, marketing, human resource management, office skills, and hospitality, leisure, sport, tourism & transport); *psychology*; *law*; *architecture, landscape architecture & design, building & planning* (including urban, rural and regional); and *education*.

Acknowledgements

All the companies participating in this project are leaders in their respective fields. While most of our interviews took place before COVID-19 resulted in social 'lockdown', some did not, and in all cases we were finalising approvals for the quotations during spring 2020. We would ordinarily be extremely grateful that such busy people gave their time to us so generously, but under the circumstances we can only record our deepest thanks to, and admiration for, all who took part while they were also involved in strategic decision-making for their companies during this extraordinary time.

The companies we include are (in alphabetical order):

1. **Cisco**
2. **Deloitte**
3. **Diageo**
4. **Gustafson, Porter + Bowman**
5. **Ipsos MORI**
6. **Royal Dutch Shell**
7. **Willis Towers Watson**
8. **WSP**

At the early stages of this project, we were particularly fortunate in having research assistance from Rory Alexander. He was meticulous in helping us gather background information about the various companies, and thoughtful in making suggestions about some interesting aspects of their work. We are grateful for his hard work and his intellectual contribution.

Finally, the Campaign for Social Science wishes, once again, to thank SAGE Publishing for sponsoring this work, and for their patience while it was completed. SAGE not only provided some of the funds to carry it out, but gave some invaluable leads to companies and interviewees, and helped design and promote the final report. SAGE has supported the Campaign in part because of its own deep commitment to the health of the social sciences and the wider contribution they make to the economy and society of the UK. We are grateful indeed for all their help.

Company: Cisco

Industry: Technology
Size: Large MNC

Website: https://www.cisco.com/
HQ: San Jose, USA

- Social sciences are used in specific projects, such as how to improve productivity or the future of work (both relevant to the COVID-19 pandemic)
- Social sciences are used to understand how to better manage ethical and privacy issues
- Social sciences are used in social problem-solving, for example through Cisco's Country Digital Acceleration programme – where innovation in health, education, and smart cities involves understanding public views, behaviours, and social/cultural contexts

Cisco is a large multinational corporation specialising in the design, production and sale of digital technologies and services. Its products are used across the world by companies, organisations, governments, and inter-governmental organisations (IGOs) to improve business functionality, stay connected across multiple locations and keep communications and data secure.[1] The company operates globally and had a turnover of $51.9 billion (USD) and 75,900 employees in 2019.[2] Whilst Cisco's technology and products focus primarily on intelligent telecom and web-based platforms with the highest levels of security and connectivity, such as Webex, they also offer supporting technical and other services.[3] Cisco's platform products are in six main areas: 'applications, data, security, cloud, infrastructure, and teams' (i.e. collaboration).[4] This case study focuses on Cisco's UK operations, which are headquartered in Feltham.

Social sciences at work

Cisco's UK staff represent a wide variety of functions, including sales, engineering, legal, marketing, communications, workplace resources (estates), and finance. The social sciences play a key role in many of these business functions.

> '*There are legal and regulatory issues that all companies must comply with. This is partly about ensuring we comply with various product standards, but it is also about social science. We have to understand the scope of law, its applicability, and ensure that we are complying with it.*'

This includes anything from using management knowledge within its human resources department, to using data to carry out market analysis, to financial planning. Cisco's legal team, for example, provides the company with the analysis and knowledge needed to navigate the differences in national legal and regulatory regimes, national and international product standards, and to remain compliant with them. Equally, Cisco's marketing team supports the company with targeted and data-driven analysis of the organisation's trends and needs, whilst also helping it to understand how new technologies can be used to achieve its goals.

> '*We have increasingly sophisticated technology, and social science skills come to the fore in helping to explain what this can do and what outcomes it can help achieve for customers. Customers need to grasp how the technology fits into their organisation's strategic plan and how to deploy it.*'

The government affairs team has members working with policy-makers in countries in each region of the world. In the UK, this has meant working on issues relating to public policy areas covering digital connectivity, skills, trade, privacy, security, innovation, sustainability, and much more.

Cisco recently published a **report** on 'The role of technology in powering an Inclusive Future'.[5] This studied the role technology has in impacting inclusiveness around the world

> '*We have used economic analysis to show government the huge variety of productivity levels across the country and the different factors that shape this – infrastructure, leadership, skills, and technology uptake. Our social science research helps inform an ongoing dialogue with government that helps us make a difference on issues that are important to us all.*'

and helped facilitate engagement with governments on policy measures that could be put in place to help drive stronger inclusiveness through more equitable access to technology. The report focused on issues like geographical, social, and gender disparities in terms of access to technology and digital connectivity.

Cisco partners with many external organisations, such as think-tanks, universities, and researchers, with a view to bringing in social science knowledge and expertise from the outside too. This was recently demonstrated by a **report** published in conjunction with the social science-led consultancy Oxford Economics, which indexes the range of productivity levels across the UK regions and seeks to understand the causes for the variation.[6]

There are, of course, many other areas where the social sciences are critical to Cisco's business, discussed below.

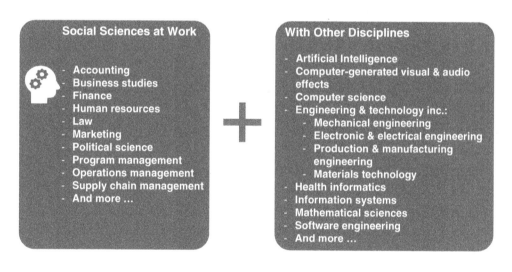

Social Sciences at Work

- Accounting
- Business studies
- Finance
- Human resources
- Law
- Marketing
- Political science
- Program management
- Operations management
- Supply chain management
- And more ...

With Other Disciplines

- Artificial Intelligence
- Computer-generated visual & audio effects
- Computer science
- Engineering & technology inc.:
  - Mechanical engineering
  - Electronic & electrical engineering
  - Production & manufacturing engineering
  - Materials technology
- Health informatics
- Information systems
- Mathematical sciences
- Software engineering
- And more ...

Social sciences working with other sciences

Cisco's work as a multinational technology business requires blending social science expertise with other sciences. For example, Cisco's work in cyber security requires bringing

'As a global business, we need to understand geopolitical risks and how the world is changing. Having people with the social science skills to help with that is important.'

> *'There is a huge benefit to having people with social science skills. We have to think about the implications that our technology will have and explain them to organisations – from realising the benefits through to managing the challenges of change. This requires input from an array of social scientists specialising in business, communications, economics, HR, law, marketing, operations, and politics to make our technology compelling.'*

together engineering and computer sciences with data sciences, business studies, and political analysis in order to help customers manage cyber threats effectively.

Another example can be seen in the increasing need for companies like Cisco to think about how people and organisations are going to use new technologies and how they will help change, for example, ways of working. This requires an understanding of what can be done with these products and services from a business, economic, political, and social perspective. A good example of this would be the technology platforms that support remote working. Innovating remote working is based not just on computer science and engineering, but an understanding of how employees will adopt and adapt to the new ways of working; and how security and data privacy is managed in this evolving environment. When technology changes the way organisations and companies work, the way meetings are run, or where people need to – or can – be based, it creates a wider structural set of sociological and societal issues for people to come to grips with, which require new HR or other strategies.

> *'From creation to design to production and launch it takes a team of engineers, plus business, marketing, and legal experts to make a product or service happen. You need a diverse team of skills to ask questions, provide different perspectives, give insight, and raise issues. To be successful, technology needs social science input.'*

For this reason, organisations will bring people together from across its different functions (e.g., communications, HR, IT, legal, marketing, and workplace resources) to help design and produce solutions with engineering. Cisco, for example, has baseline company policies (like human rights

Social Scientists on Staff

- Business management
- Finance and accounting
- Government affairs
- Human resources
- Legal
- Marketing
- Program management
- Operations management
- Supply chain management
- And more...

'We strive to have a diverse group of people working in our organisation. It's important to have employees from different backgrounds and with experiences.'

and privacy rules) that have to be complied with on all new products and services in addition to specific requirements.

Social scientists on staff

Social science skills are valuable for many of the roles for which Cisco hires, whether through its graduate scheme or other routes. The broader support functions like HR, legal, marketing, operations, and professional services, for example, need social scientists who are lawyers, marketing experts, HR experts, management experts in supply chain, strategy and logistics, and business experts.

Acknowledging that university isn't for everyone, alongside existing recruitment methods, Cisco has an apprenticeship programme in the UK, where participants spend three years exploring a variety of roles within Cisco and receive a BSc in Digital and Technology Solutions upon completion. Cisco is keen to encourage people with a diverse range of backgrounds and skills to apply for jobs in that programme, and across the company.

Social impact

Cisco's technology enables businesses, charities, communities, government departments, and IGOs to safely and securely embrace digital ways of working. This has enabled major innovations in how organisations work and has helped drive inclusivity. Cisco's technology has become increasingly important during the COVID-19 global pandemic, as a large proportion of the population has suddenly found themselves reliant on technologies that allow them to work – and teach and study – from home. To help keep people working, the company has 'been providing free offerings and cloud-based services across Webex, and security solutions that have kept newly-remote workforces running productively'.[7]

The company has also committed a total of $225 million (USD) to help respond to COVID-19, which includes '$8 million in cash and $210 million in product', and is focused on 'supporting healthcare, education, government response and critical technology for organisations like the United Nations, the World Health Organisation, and non-profits in 180 countries'. And, through their Country Digital Acceleration (CDA) programme, Cisco is also 'providing funding for heads of state, government agencies and businesses to rapidly deploy technology solutions' to help this transformative shift to digital working, living and governance.[8]

Cisco's CDA programme invests in innovation projects in various countries to demonstrate technological benefits in different settings. It is 'a long-term partnership with national leadership, industry and aca-

> *'From a social science perspective, it's about the positive impact that technology has and the opportunity it presents to organisations.'*

> *'Social skills are needed to explain what our technology does, especially as technology becomes more automated. The value we will bring is in the relationship; understanding what an organisation is interested in, engaging with them, and building the relationship.'*

demia' and hopes that 'by accelerating the national digitisation agenda, the country can then grow GDP, create new jobs and provide innovation and education across the public and private sectors'.[9]

So far, the programme has helped advance health sector innovation, deliver smart cities and, through its 5G Rural First project, deploy 5G to the UK's most under-served communities. Cisco has also created a global network of 12 Co-Innovation Centres that 'work with regional and global partners to create new technology solutions that solve industry pain points and positively impact business, society and the planet.'[10] Cisco also works with the NHS to help provide innovative solutions for healthcare delivery and on issues like better ageing. These often need to integrate the insights of social sciences from behavioural economics to social work and policy.[11] Cisco, for example, recently carried out a project on behavioural economics with the NHS – using smart technology to incentivise people to walk an extra bus stop past their normal stop, for increased health benefit.

Looking forward

In 2017, Cisco partnered with Oxford Economics (OE) to report on the future of work, and the impact of AI on jobs and the type of work that people will be doing in the future.[12] Combining Cisco's expertise in data and computer science with OE's understanding of economics and society, they were able to better understand how AI could change jobs in the future and what implications that may have for employers. A key finding was that whilst 'there are acute ICT skills shortfall to overcome ... paradoxically, as technology becomes more capable it is

'Technology plays a pivotal role in evolving the world of work and we must be cognisant of the impact that it has. This is so we can work with organisations to develop strategies as they navigate a new way of working and adopt and adapt to the technology rather than reject it. That's why social science research is so important in technology evolution.'

'We don't just sell technology we help to develop organisations, so we must understand the impact the technology will have on them. That entails having social science skills that you can apply to understand an organisation's challenge and help to solve it.'

"human skills" that explain much of the gap between today's workforce and the needs of the future.'

Social science knowledge and insights are increasingly important for Cisco, and for other companies like it that are investing heavily in R&D in order to develop new technologies. This is because companies need to understand not only the technology itself, but also how it is going to be used, and how it may be received in society. Whether a new piece of technology is aimed at new ways of working collaboratively with colleagues, new ways of digitising and automating work processes, or new ways of automating factory functions, companies need to understand the legal, HR, regulatory, ethical, and political issues that may arise from it for long-term success, and ethical conduct.

Notes

1 Bureau van Dijk (2020, April 9) Cisco Systems company report: Industry & Activities. BvD ID no. US770059951. Retrieved from https://orbis.bvdep.com.
2 Bureau van Dijk, Cisco Systems company report: Key Information.
3 Bureau van Dijk, Cisco Systems company report: Industry & Activities.
4 https://www.cisco.com/c/dam/en_us/about/annual-report/cisco-annual-report-2019.pdf.
5 Cisco (2020) The role of technology in powering an Inclusive Future. https://www.cisco.com/c/dam/m/en_us/about/cxo-agenda/inclusive-future/the-role-of-technology-in-powering-an-inclusive-future.pdf.
6 https://www.cisco.com/c/m/en_uk/productivity-index.html.
7 https://www.cisco.com/c/m/en_us/covid19/letter-to-customers-partners.html.
8 https://blogs.cisco.com/news/committing-225-million-to-global-covid-19-response.
9 https://newsroom.cisco.com/cda.
10 https://www.cisco.com/c/en/us/solutions/innovation-centers.html#~case-studies.
11 See, e.g.: https://www.cisco.com/c/dam/global/en_uk/solutions/industries/public-sector/government-new/jl_thinking_digitally_about_health_and_care_digital.pdf; or https://www.cisco.com/c/en_uk/solutions/industries/healthcare.html.
12 https://www.cisco.com/c/dam/assets/csr/pdf/The-AI-Paradox-How-Robots-Will-Make-Work-More-Human.pdf. See also: https://www.oxfordeconomics.com/recent-releases/the-AI-paradox.

Company: Deloitte

Industry: Accounting & Business Services
Size: Large Enterprise

Website: www2.deloitte.com
HQ: London, UK

- Social sciences used in consultancy – often involving economics and other social science knowledge and skills, like geography or understanding behavioural change
- Social sciences are used in accountancy, law, business, and management functions that often require both specific technical skills and wider social science input
- Social sciences underpin the design and analysis of Deloitte's Chief Financial Officer survey, used by a range of policy-makers, including the Bank of England and Treasury

Deloitte is one of the 'big four' global accounting firms, and a world-leading business services firm, headquartered in the UK. It employs over 16,500 people in the UK, and over 300,000 professionals globally.[1] Deloitte's revenue is over £3 billion in the UK,[2] and about £35 billion worldwide in 2019.[3] The company provides professional services in the broad areas of: audit and assurance; consulting; financial advice for mergers and acquisitions; legal, private equity and family enterprise; risk advisory; and tax services. Its work affects a wide range of sectors in the economy, including consumer (e.g., automotive, retail, transport); energy, resources and industrial (e.g., construction, mining, oil and gas, utilities); financial services (e.g., banking, capital markets, insurance); government and public services (e.g., health and social care, defence, transport, civil service); life sciences and healthcare; and technology, media and telecommunications. Deloitte's clients are mostly other businesses, but its clients also include policy-makers (such as the UK government and some of its departments) and many third-sector organisations.

Social sciences at work

The services that Deloitte provides to other businesses, institutions and governments draw heavily on a wide variety of social sciences. Audit and tax services, for example, use accountancy. The consulting division draws on the knowledge that comes from business and management studies. Legal services require a deep understanding of the law and legal research; financial advisory will draw on a deeper understanding of finance and accounting studies; and risk advisory uses knowledge from the disciplines of politics, law, and operations management – to name but a few.

In this case study, we use the example of Deloitte's macro-economics team. Economics is itself a social science, and the team draws on the disciplinary knowledge of its staff to conduct daily tasks like analysis, commentary, and reporting on macroeconomic trends in developed and major emerging

'We analyse a lot of information, using history, economics, and a broader knowledge of business to process data into messaging that is easy to absorb. The objective is to condense vast amounts of information into the most important themes that our clients or policy makers should consider.'

market economies – as well as major themes (like the future of work), to help clients understand the economic environments they operate in and how they might look in future. When producing some strategic analyses, it will draw not only upon its members' own disciplinary expertise, but may also include insights from outside economists and other social science academics. For example, Baroness Wolf came to speak at Deloitte about how the vocational education sector has evolved over the last 20 years, and what the consequences of that could be for the firm and its clients. To better understand global trends, the team will also combine their economic analyses and understanding with insight from other social sciences. For instance, they may draw upon studies in history, and human and social geography to understand regional or international differences, or look at a wide variety of disciplines to understand behavioural change when companies are considering how to be more inclusive of women workers or an ageing workforce.

Social sciences working with other sciences

Deloitte's work also often requires teams with multidisciplinary backgrounds and the use of multidisciplinary approaches. For example, some of the impact cases highlighted in its annual reports are work the company has done to reduce waiting times for NHS operations through co-design of a new booking system using AI,[4] and speeding up the mobilisation of Save the Children's emergency response teams.[5] As with so many of today's challenges, the blending of social science insight with technology can create significant synergies for faster and more effective delivery of things like healthcare or disaster relief. Another good example of this type of collaboration between social science and technical knowledge is the collaboration between Deloitte and Dr Carl Frey (an economist and economic historian) and Dr Michael Osbourne (Associate Professor of Machine Learning) at Oxford University on a **report** assessing the jobs that are most at risk of automation in the UK[6] – which helped improve the firm's understanding of the UK labour market, and also of the kind of skills and jobs that may or may not exist in the future.

Social scientists on staff

There are a number of trained social scientists on staff across the company involved in the direct delivery of services. In addition to the obvious accountants, finance graduates, lawyers, and business and management graduates (with

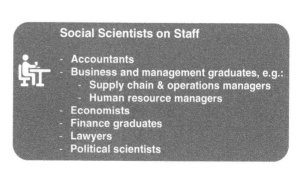

specialist knowledge ranging from supply chain and organisational management to human resources), there are, for example, those with degrees in political science and economics.

> '*Hiring practices vary across different divisions within Deloitte. In general the people hired are reasonably numerate with strong problem-solving skills, no matter what degree they did at university. But we increasingly value empathy, social skills, and judgement. The ability to form a reasoned opinion, often without complete or well-structured information, as most real-life situations demand – that is key to our jobs.*'

In order to diversify its workforce and increase the range of perspectives within its staff, the company does not require specific degrees for recruitment but has a minimum skills requirement and on-line assessment process. A strong apprenticeship programme has also been introduced to find people with such an aptitude outside of the university system. This means that the company is prepared to provide in-house training, for example with accounting and corporate finance accreditation, to help those from other disciplines gain that type of expertise. Three out of five members of Deloitte's UK-based macroeconomics team, for example, have degrees purely in economics, one has degrees in both physics and applied microeconomics, and another in linguistics. The approach is to hire bright, hard-working people and then give them the business knowledge that might be required.

Those who can combine a high degree of data and numeracy skills with the type of critical reasoning skills often found in social science graduates are particularly sought after. Critical reasoning and the ability to make judgements from social contexts and data are vital skills; for example, accountants may be asked to pair their disciplinary knowledge with knowledge about

> '*You expect a certain level of confidence and competence in analysing both quantitative and qualitative data from social scientists. You also expect the ability to quickly develop an understanding of the history and the context of the situation being studied ... and a level of ease and experience, in weighing all possible arguments and making a reasoned, defensible judgement.*'

particular areas of society. As the world changes, accountancy is no longer a cut-and-dried measuring of profit and loss, as many line items previously seen as costs are now seen as investments. This is true for tech companies, for example, in areas like intellectual property research or branding, which in the past was seen as a marketing cost. Now such expenditures are increasingly seen as an investment. Making such a determination requires judgement, and an understanding of the broader business picture.

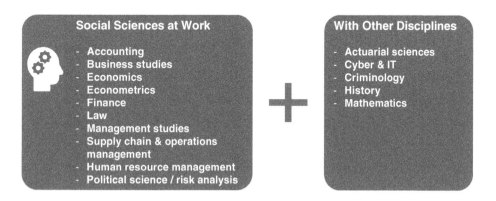

Social Sciences at Work

- Accounting
- Business studies
- Economics
- Econometrics
- Finance
- Law
- Management studies
- Supply chain & operations management
- Human resource management
- Political science / risk analysis

With Other Disciplines

- Actuarial sciences
- Cyber & IT
- Criminology
- History
- Mathematics

Social impact

Professional services provided by firms like Deloitte use social science skills and knowledge to help UK businesses and other organisations in areas such as accountancy, tax advice, legal services, or investment advice. Deloitte also helps a wide range of clients find solutions and answers to pressing issues and priority challenges they may face in today's changing environment. Its annual impact report highlights the company's work with private companies and public partners (including local and national governments) on issues ranging 'from the climate emergency to the productivity puzzle'.[7] In response to the recent public debate over the role of audit and assurance in society (which makes up a portion of its business), Deloitte is 'supporting reform and meaningful change as part of the Government and industry reviews'.[8] The firm has also worked on over 300 different projects in the last three years to help companies prepare for Brexit, whether that be helping to ensure that they had the right management plan to handle upcoming changes in their supply chains, or preparing for the regulatory and tax changes ahead.[9]

Insights from the social sciences can have strong impact on broad policy and the navigation of challenging times. Deloitte's macroeconomics team, for example, tracks a broad range of issues that aid both business and government decision-making.

The Deloitte CFO Survey, established just before the financial crisis, is regularly used by policy-makers in institutions such as the Bank of England, the Treasury and other government departments, to inform their views on business sentiment, credit conditions, and corporate decision-making. During the credit crunch, the survey was an authoritative barometer of financing conditions for the UK's largest, most international businesses, with preliminary findings provided to the Bank of England's Monetary Policy Committee before its rate-setting meetings. More recently, the survey has been used by policy-makers to assess how corporations have responded to elevated levels of uncertainty due to Brexit, the COVID-19 crisis and weaker global growth. The survey findings are also used by Deloitte's clients, and Deloitte itself, to assess sentiment in the broader corporate sector and its willingness to take risks and make major investments, to support strategic planning.

Looking forward

An example of this strategic perspective is another recent Deloitte **report** on automation that showed that the jobs that have seen the highest growth over the last two decades, and the skills that have been in greatest demand, have been those based on creativity, social skills, and empathy. It found that 'a strong pattern through time is that tasks that are repetitive and routine for humans are increasingly performed by machines ... Meanwhile thousands of new jobs are being created every year in technology and creative occupations, business and professional services, and caring professions. These jobs require a high degree of manual dexterity or cognitive skills – a further shift from brawn to brains.'[10]

Notes

1 https://www2.deloitte.com/uk/en/pages/about-deloitte-uk/articles/who-we-are.
   html;

2 https://www.accountancydaily.co/deloitte-uk-revenues-11-partner-profits-hit-ps882k.

3 https://www2.deloitte.com/global/en/pages/about-deloitte/articles/global-revenue-
   announcement.html.

4 https://www2.deloitte.com/uk/en/pages/impact-report-2019/stories/heart-of-the-
   matter.html.

5 https://www2.deloitte.com/uk/en/pages/impact-report-2019/foreword.html.

6 Deloitte (2014) London Futures: Agiletown: the relentless march of technology and London's
   response.   https://www2.deloitte.com/content/dam/Deloitte/uk/Documents/uk-
   futures/london-futures-agiletown.pdf.

7 https://www2.deloitte.com/uk/en/pages/impact-report-2019/foreword.html.

8 https://www2.deloitte.com/uk/en/pages/impact-report-2019/stories/the-audit-
   debate.html.

9 https://www2.deloitte.com/uk/en/pages/impact-report-2019/stories/brexit.html.

10 https://www2.deloitte.com/content/dam/Deloitte/uk/Documents/Growth/deloitte-
    uk-insights-from-brawns-to-brain.pdf.

Company: Diageo

Industry: Manufacturing & Retail (Consumer Products)

Size: Large MNC

Website: https://www.diageo.com/

HQ: London, UK

- Social sciences are essential to understand consumer behaviour and market demographics
- Social sciences are used in public policy engagement, to promote responsible alcohol use and improvements in sustainability
- Social sciences are essential to promote long-term change in addressing supply and environmental issues, for example where specific country expertise is vital

Diageo is a large multinational manufacturing and retail consumer products firm producing alcoholic beverages, headquartered in the UK. Diageo employs almost 30,000 people across 30 countries in five regions (North America, Europe and Turkey, Asia Pacific, Africa and Latin America). It reported an operating profit of over **£4 billion in 2019.** Diageo produces over 200 brands of alcohol from beer (like Guinness) to Scotch whisky (like Johnny Walker), sold in more than 180 countries. Diageo has several operating divisions, including: (1) Supply, which makes and delivers the company's products to distributors, wholesalers, restaurants/pubs and consumers; (2) Sales; (3) Procurement, which can range from sourcing raw ingredients (from farmers large and small) and logistics to hedging the price risks for commodities in the company's supply chain; (4) Marketing; (5) Legal; (6) Information Services; (7) Human Resources; (8) Finance; (9) Corporate Relations; and (10) Global Business Services. The social sciences play a role in each of these functions. The governance, including regulation

> *'If you look at our internal value chain you see a lot of room for social scientists, through marketing and sales all the way through the production and our global programmes on education.'*

and taxation, within which Diageo operates is set both by policy-makers and wider consumer attitudes.

Social sciences at work

The social sciences play an invaluable role across Diageo's business. They are not just in the obvious areas that require business, finance, account-ancy, and legal knowledge, though all of these are essential to the everyday functioning of the firm. The social sciences are also important throughout the business's many functions, because the company's success requires a deep understanding of consumer behaviour and market demographics, in the context of relevant regulation. The social sciences play a particularly important role, for example, in helping Diageo set the company's strategy, not just in ensuring the robust data needed to make decisions. This also requires bringing together data from STEM and the social sciences to consider issues like adapting to climate change and ensuring sustainable water use – while other issues requiring social science include matters such as changes in consumer behaviour, changing social regulation, and public policy.

> 'When evolving the strategy of the company, we absolutely need to have expertise in our employee base that draws on all of the disciplines of the social sciences, and to take expert advice and sounding from the outside world to challenge our thinking and help it evolve.'

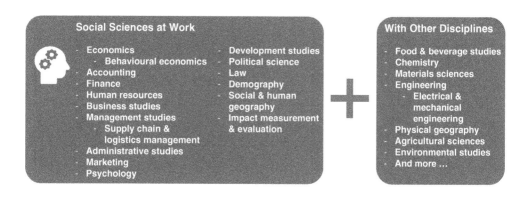

Social Sciences at Work		With Other Disciplines
- Economics - Behavioural economics - Accounting - Finance - Human resources - Business studies - Management studies - Supply chain & logistics management - Administrative studies - Marketing - Psychology	- Development studies - Political science - Law - Demography - Social & human geography - Impact measurement & evaluation	- Food & beverage studies - Chemistry - Materials sciences - Engineering - Electrical & mechanical engineering - Physical geography - Agricultural sciences - Environmental studies - And more ...

Consumer behaviour/insights

Production, marketing, and sales all require insight into the consumer: what do they want when they make purchasing decisions, and what influences those decisions? A range of social science disciplines, including psychology and behavioural economics, help Diageo better understand the consumer and how to meet changing demand. Behavioural psychology, for example, is increasingly important to the company, as it seeks to use the lessons of the nudge effect (getting people to make better choices by changing their default choices) to encourage people to drink in a more moderate way.

> '*Whether you are in marketing, running a sales team, or in innovation and you are trying to think about R&D, you need to understand the consumer. There is no point in doing R&D as a consumer goods company unless that R&D is guided by consumer insights. So again, we need STEM people to help us manufacture, we need the chemical scientists and the liquid scientists to help us make our products, we need technologists who help with things like production and storage ... but there is no point in doing all of that, if you haven't got anyone to sell to, because you have ignored what the consumers are telling you and the insights they give you.*'

A clear example of this is the company's work to tackle the issue of 'free pouring', particularly in rich countries. When consumers order a drink in a bar or restaurant, the drink is measured, but at home 'free' (or unmeasured) pouring can lead people to drink more than they realise. Using the insights from behavioural psychology, Diageo now fits optics into the necks of many of its products to help consumers understand what is a single versus a larger serving and, in that way, nudge home consumers towards moderation.

Public policy

A firm understanding of public policy (with insights from the disciplines of political science, social policy, and law) is critical for Diageo. This is in part because alcohol is a unique substance, which is commonly consumed but which, if misused, can also be dangerous. Diageo takes this corporate responsibility very seriously. It also includes a broader responsibility faced by all companies, to ensure wise actions in the face of climate change, water use, and other environmental and community issues. For instance, Diageo's products require water, and this requires special care in many parts of the world if Diageo is to be a sustainable and responsible business. Another example is the issue of plastics use. Policy-makers rightly wish companies like Diageo to reduce their carbon emissions, but while they can reduce them on a science-based basis, there are trade-offs. Scotch whisky, for example, is a quarter of Diageo's business and needs to be made and bottled in Scotland in order to be considered 'Scotch' whisky. Using glass rather than plastic bottles in this process comes with trade-offs, because glass bottles are heavy and carry a correspondingly heavy carbon cost to ship across the world. Making responsible changes requires detailed consideration and working with government on optimal solutions.

> 'There is little point in us trying to change the environmental or social footprint of the company in a way that policy-makers do not wish us to. We need to interface with policy-makers – they need to understand what we are trying to achieve, and we need to understand what they want us to do. It is an iterative process. It takes skill and understanding to help policy-makers understand some of the tradeoffs we face in reaching our commitments – and that is really valuable. We also need to understand what they expect, and how they will regulate us or tax us to change our behaviour. So social science insights into public policy are absolutely critical.'

Economics

Many parts of Diageo's business create a strong demand for economists. Issues include export taxation, domestic taxation, and regulation. As a result, Diageo needs economic modelling of potential national strategies for raising revenue and public health, and to make the case for optimal legislation.

Social sciences working with other sciences

As with many of the companies that we look at in this report, Diageo needs both social scientists and those with knowledge of STEM to work together towards the common goal of their business's success.

> 'For a company like ours, who are partly a big manufacturer, STEM is important – but that doesn't mean that other things aren't important too.'

For example, social science experts in supply chain management will work closely with those experts in the food and beverage and materials sciences to ensure that the best products are delivered to consumers in a sustainable and efficient way. Development studies and public policy specialists will work together with food and beverage scientists to ensure that the raw materials used in these products are produced in a responsible way that respects human rights and helps lift up communities within their supply chains, while producing the best inputs possible for the company's products.

Social scientists on staff

Roughly 30,000 people work directly for Diageo. Around 20,000 of those are on the manufacturing/supply side, where there is naturally a greater need for more graduates with STEM degrees. Among the other 10,000 or so globally that work on the 'demand side' – the part of the company that works on getting products to the consumer – there is a huge demand for

> 'If you break down different functions in the company there will almost always be a subset of people with social science degrees — some of whom we will have actively sought out, like the economists or the lawyers or those working on consumer insights or consumer research, and then some of whom just happen to have that background and we think that is good because it gives us a diverse employee base and a well-educated one.'

people with various social science degrees. In Diageo's headquarters operations, for example, human resources is particularly interested in those with knowledge of psychology and policy management skills (for the reasons discussed above), and generally seeks to bring in people from many of the social science disciplines to work across many HQ functions. In the company's finance teams, accountants, MBAs, economists and so on, are critical. High-quality lawyers are required because Diageo is a highly regulated business. In corporate relations, which also looks at how the company is regulated and the company's environmental and social impact, there is a strong need for those with social science knowledge and skills, from economists through to behavioural scientists and public policy specialists. Almost everyone who works in corporate relations, for example, will have a graduate or a higher degree, and most of these are in the social sciences. Marketing requires people with deep knowledge not only of marketing and business studies, but also importantly those with knowledge and understanding of psychology. Development studies experts are also important because Diageo has a large operational presence in the developing world and, while some operational issues are broadly the same across countries, others are highly location-specific.

Social Scientists on Staff

- Lawyers
- Finance & accounting experts
- Business experts
- Management experts
  - Supply chain management experts
  - Human resource management experts
- Economists
- Marketing experts
- Political scientists
- Development experts
- Demographers
- Measurement & evaluation experts

Social impact

Diageo takes seriously its responsibility to educate the public about how to use its products safely and responsibly at an appropriate age, in addition to its other environmental and social commitments as a large employer and consumer manufacturer. But Diageo believes there is no point in putting money, time, and effort into these programmes if they don't work.

Most of the programmes Diageo runs tend to be focused on the hardest thing to achieve – changing human behaviour for the long term to avoid harm. Diageo increasingly relies on social science to ensure robust measurement and evaluation of the impact of its projects. Sometimes this will take place in-house, and sometimes the company will commission evaluations from academics. Their award-winning programme 'Smashed',[1] for example, teaches children and parents why it is important to follow drinking age limits, by using role play to show children the effects of drinking, and the harm to the human body and in social interactions caused by underage drinking. Run through an NGO in 23 countries and growing, it has now reached 700,000 young people on six continents over the last ten years,'[2] using robust social science knowledge of measurement and evaluation to ensure that parents and children change their behaviours, and that the programme is delivering change in return for the investment.

In addition to their programmes on tackling alcohol harm, Diageo runs numerous community programmes on issues like water use and woman's empowerment. A good example of the use of social sciences to work for change in society is Diageo's 'Glass is Good' initiative in Brazil. Most of the company's products are shipped in glass bottles, but recycling by hand can be dangerous for workers and bottle collection difficult. Using expertise on reverse supply chain logistics, the company's 'Glass is Good' initiative works to collect bottles and bring them to recyclers that have been outfitted with machine-operated glass-breaking hammermills to recycle over 60 tons of glass per month in the country.[3] Not only is this producing a more environmentally sustainable supply chain, but it also helps increase income for those working in the recycling cooperatives in Brazil.

Looking forward

Diageo is currently setting its next decade of social and environmental commitments for 2030 in line with the UN's Sustainable Development Goals (SDGs). These include both hard environmental commitments – for example, getting to net positive on climate change, lowering the environmental impact of packaging and working towards becoming a circular economy company – as well as social commitments and community investments. When setting these types of commitments, companies like Diageo must first identify

> *'Again, we can't do this kind of strategic and agenda-setting work without people who understand social sciences, like public policy, development studies, or human geography.'*

opportunities and risks, such as the changing nature of work and the rise of AI. The social sciences play a significant role in this. Expertise in public policy, development, human geography, and economics help Diageo make achievable social and environmental commitments.

Notes

1   http://smashedproject.org/an-international-project/.

2   https://www.diageo.com/en/in-society/promoting-positive-drinking/.

3   https://www.diageo.com/en/news-and-media/videos/diageo-brazil-glass-is-good-recycling-project/.

- Social sciences are used in understanding how people use public spaces and what makes for successful development outcomes, going beyond economics
- Social sciences are used in understanding the local social, cultural, and economic history of areas for development
- Social sciences knowledge and skills are used, for instance, in designing public consultations, experimenting with signage, etc.

Gustafson Porter + Bowman (GP + B) is an award-winning London-based landscape architecture practice whose work includes public realm development projects at home and across the globe, creating socially and environmentally beneficial spaces for communities and their visitors. It is a small to medium sized enterprise (SME) with around 30 staff and a turnover of about £3 million. The practice's work is in six main categories: (1) *culture and heritage* work, such as the Diana, Princess of Wales Memorial Fountain and the re-design of the Eiffel Tower site; (2) *parks and gardens*, such as their design for Parque Central in Valencia; (3) *infrastructure and city masterplans*, like the redevelopment of the centre of York; (4) *plazas*, like London's King's Cross Square; (5) *residential*, like the Chelsea Barracks, and (6) other large-scale *public realm* projects like Shoreditch Village or Rotterdam's Museumpark.

> '*The big question we are trying to answer is: How do you get people to change their behaviour in an urban environment?*'

Social sciences at work

GP + B's work explores how social behaviours relate to, and can be affected by, the built environment. How close somebody wants to be to another person, or how fast people move, depends on social and cultural norms, so that these will often be different in the UK from those in the United States, Asia, or Africa. GP + B often works with water, for example, because empirical evidence shows that it can be a great attractor. Even when placing a bench, GP + B must look at factors like proximity to walkways that may affect whether people feel comfortable using it. All of these sorts of behavioural habits inform GP + B's work – and while some of this is intuitive, much of it is learned through professional practice of what works and what doesn't work, which is often underpinned by evidence.

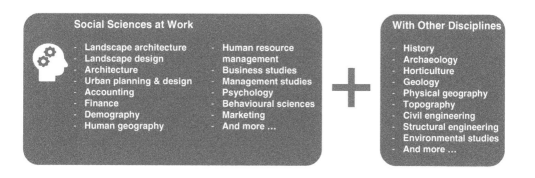

Social sciences working with other sciences

When developing a project, GP + B apply social science and other skills and knowledge to research the cultural and environmental history of the site, in order to explore the potential for regeneration, and to be able to ensure the social relevance and sustainability of the project. This includes understanding the cultural, archaeological, economic, and social history of a site, while also engaging with its physical geography, topology, and geology. They also look at the demography and behavioural patterns of the surrounding population – using discipline-specific knowledge and skills from the social and other sciences to understand and model how different groups use the space now, what their future behavioural trends may be, and how they may want to use that space in the future. This means not only engaging with experts from signage to psychology, but also carrying out extensive public consultations to improve the effect of the project site on the local community, using established social science methodologies for surveys, data collection, modelling, and forecasting.

GP + B's work thus requires multidisciplinary approaches and teams to undertake a single project. In some cases, projects will be led by an architect or engineer, and GP + B will form part of the multidisciplinary team that is engaged, but when a specific project is primarily focused on the landscape, GP + B will lead the project and collaborate with a multidisciplinary team underneath them. A good example of the latter is GP + B's recent redesign of the Eiffel Tower site, where the practice is the lead landscape architect, with 28 sub- and co-consultants, including architects, engineers, civil engineers, branding consultants, experts in signage, lighting, business, finance, soil, acoustics, pedestrian modelling, and transport, and even advisors on economics and business strategy to help improve the commercial value of the site.

Social scientists on staff

Architecture, landscape architecture, landscape design, building, and planning include social science knowledge because they bring social considerations together with the built environment to create optimal spaces in which people live, work, and social-

Social Scientists on Staff

- Landscape architects
- Landscape designers
- Architects
- Urban planners / designers
- Finance / accountants
- Human resource managers

ise. GP + B's practice employs around 30 people, most of whom are architects or landscape architects, but who also include specialists in areas like horticulture and water. They also employ accountants and managers to help run their business. On each project they team up with a wider range and number of social and other scientists to scope and deliver their projects, who might range from engineers in the hard sciences,

> *'We want to create comfort conditions for people in an external landscape, so we look at things like sun and shadow, and where people want to sit. But we also work with people who specialise in pedestrian modelling, people flow, and behaviour modification… just as we will with people who help with cost planning and business planning, and a wider vision for systems for social change.'*

to historians in the arts and humanities, to behavioural scientists in the social sciences. They often work, for example, with social scientists in companies like **Space Syntax** or **Movement Strategies**, who use open source data on behavioural movement to track where people are going to and from in order to conduct pedestrian modelling for places and big events – allowing GP + B to create spaces that improve these flows for people and their environments.

Social impact

When done well, landscape architecture and design can improve public life and wellbeing. It can help cities achieve goals for sustainability, equality, and safety by, for example, helping to lower rates of anti-social

> *'We look at patterns, at what people want to see in their communities, and then work together with local government to make that happen.'*

> *'We look at how you can turn these post-industrial towns into new business areas and regenerate around the natural assets that are already there.'*

behaviour, increase inclusion, and find solutions to urban problems like pedestrian and vehicular traffic congestion.

GP + B support government management teams to prepare strategic economic and development plans for large public realm projects, which entails the need to understand the potential of a site and to identify issues ranging from capacity and accessibility, to safety and inclusion.

For example, when working on a masterplan for a town with an industrial heritage, GP + B examine its existing natural and human resources to help the town build a plan for the next 20 years. This type of work entails having access to technical social and other scientific knowledge and skills in order to marry discipline-specific knowledge and skills in landscape architecture and design with a wider understanding of the social, geographical, and economic context of a project. It also requires building good relationships with local governments, communities, and academic institutions.

Looking forward

The work landscape architects do is becoming more widely recognised, particularly in terms of its ability to help society deal with climate change, and the wider environmental issues and behavioural responses the UK now faces.

'Landscape architecture is a broader discipline than people realise, and I believe it can grow further and tackle the big issues that we face with climate change and environmental change. As a discipline, we can be in a position to understand not only the environmental challenges ahead, but also the social and cultural changes that will take place in the future.'

Company: Ipsos MORI

Industry: Market Research
Size: Medium-sized Enterprise

Website: www.ipsos-mori.com
HQ: London, UK

- Social science knowledge and skills are essential to understand consumer behaviours and views
- Social science knowledge and skills are the basis for designing and conducting robust surveys and other measures of people's behaviour and attitudes
- Social science knowledge and skills are essential in conducting and understanding citizen and public sector research, whether through opinion polls, evaluations of government programmes, or research into social trends

Ipsos MORI is a global market research and public opinion polling company, with a turnover of over €134 million and over 1,200 employees in 2018.[1] It is the UK-based subsidiary of Ipsos SA, which is one of the largest market research firms in the world,[2] with over 5,000 clients in 90 markets,[3] and a turnover of $2.26 billion and 18,417 employees in 2019.[4] Ipsos (and Ipsos MORI) offers 17 distinct services to clients: *audience measurement*; *innovation*; *retail and consumer intelligence*; *brand health tracking*; *clinics and mobility labs*; *market strategy and understanding*; *creative excellence*; *mystery shopping*; *corporate reputation*; *observer*; *customer experience*; *public affairs*; *healthcare*; *social intelligence analytics*; *quality measurement*; *Ipsos Marketing Management & Analytics (MMA)*; *Ipsos UU* (qualitative research); as well as other services.[5] Ipsos MORI offers a wide range of quantitative and qualitative research for its clients – who

> 'Our strapline here is 'total understanding,' and you can only get total understanding if you understand people as consumers, as citizens, as voters, as men and women or non-binary ... as human beings. You have to understand that people in those different states and in those different moments are different, and what that means for your customers and their product or policies.'

range from the UK government to large industrial and technology companies to small start-ups around the globe – all of whom want to understand better the markets in which they operate and the people they are trying to reach within them.

Social sciences at work

> 'We are a social science business. Many of our employees are social scientists and we are a successful commercial business that uses social science to deliver for our clients – but we also use social science skills to help run our business, which is slightly different.'

Ipsos MORI's business is social science research – in other words it uses social science research methods (quantitative and qualitative) from different disciplines to find information (data) about targeted elements of society (particular markets) for its clients, and then analyse that information using social science (again from many different disciplines) to provide insights to its clients in response to particular questions or problems. However, social science also informs almost every aspect of how its own business is run, and is used to make decisions about everything from hiring to its long-term business strategy.

Social sciences as a business

The largest division at Ipsos MORI is its **public affairs** business, covering many teams aimed at supporting the public sector through research and opinion tracking on substantive issues ranging from employment and skills, crime and justice, government and society, to faith and social cohesion. They use a variety of survey methods to conduct political and opinion polling, using knowledge from political science, econometrics, sociology, psychology, and social and public policy. They have a **behavioural research group** that helps develop and evaluate behavioural interventions, drawing on social sciences like psychology, sociology, and behavioural economics.

They have a **policy and evaluation research team** that 'leads a range of evaluation projects for UK, European and international clients across the public and not-for-profit sectors … conducting robust social research across the full spectrum of policy areas to deliver high quality and impactful end-to-end evaluations, drawing on knowledge from political science, public and social policy, economics, and specialists in evaluation methods'. Perhaps most well known is their **Social Research Institute**, whose experts in social science methods and in social and public policy 'develop and carry out customised research for clients in the government and public sector to help them make better, evidence-based decisions'.

Social science to run and support the business

'We use social science methodologies to achieve our goals in each area of our business plan. Social science helps us make decisions about our own business and it informs how we work.'

The social sciences are also used to help run and support its business. Ipsos MORI's *operational effectiveness* activities look at automation, data science, and managing resources effectively within the business. This requires an understanding of automation principles and how they can be sensibly applied, as well as understanding economics. The *profitable growth* strand looks at market areas in which the business may wish to expand, as well as whether the company is being run effectively and profitably – again relying on disciplines like economics and finance. The *client-related* strand focuses on interaction with clients — surveying them and speaking to them on a regular

'All of the functions in our business use either an understanding of economics or social research – or use people who do economics, social research, or some other type of research for a living – to inform our business decisions, for example around our resourcing models or how we prioritise things. It is all done using social science logic. So social science runs through everything we do to a greater or a lesser extent.'

basis to monitor their satisfaction with Ipsos MORI's services through-out the contract cycle. The *impact strand* of its business plan focuses on efforts to make a contribution back to society, more broadly through its social research. Ipsos MORI, for example, runs its own thought leadership activities which go beyond reputation building, to help improve society – looking at issues such as how to improve the life experience of women and girls.

Finally, the social sciences are particularly important for inform-ing Ipsos MORI's *people-related* activities. Its human resources department, for example, uses social sciences in numerous ways, from the gender pay gap analysis produced by its 'people' team, to the listening events the company holds across the busi-ness to understand how staff are feeling, to let them know they are valued, and to keep them engaged. It also deploys social science knowledge in its own

> '*We try to make the most of the people that we employ – our social scientists – to enhance the HR offer at Ipsos. We use our behavioural scientists to look at our job descriptions. We use our employee experience researchers to look at our employee journey. We work with the people that work in our social intelligence analytics team to look at how we can use data to make better decisions about how we are recruiting and attracting people into our business.*'

learning, drawing on its internal resources of social scientists from a variety of disciplines, such as social data analysts to behavioural scientists. For instance, it

> '*Social science is actually embedded in everything we do in HR. We use social science to attract talent into the organisation, and to make that a better process that gives us the right result. The right result is hiring the right people (behaviourally and cognitively) into our organisation.*'

draws on the external expertise of occupational psychologists to help with designing the psycho-metric tests used as part of the company's graduate recruitment programme, to ensure the best behavioural fit (with the compa-ny's values) and cognitive fit (with the skills and capabilities required for the position).

Social Sciences at Work

- Marketing
- Sociology
- Economics
- Behavioral economics
- Social research
- Psychology
- Geography
- Political science
- Political polling
- Social policy
- Human resources

- Management studies
- Business studies
- Ethnography
- Anthropology
- And more ...

+

Data Science

With Other Disciplines

- Mathematics
- Statistics
- Information technology
- Computer science
- History
- Graphic design
- Art
- Filmography
- Communications
- Semiotics
- Neuroscience
- And more ...

Social sciences working with other disciplines

Market research as an industry has changed dramatically in the last 40 years. In the 1980s, market research focused primarily on surveys conducted through focus groups, face to face interviews, postal surveys, or by telephone – and communication channels were limited to outlets like TV, radio, billboards, mainstream press, or mailings sent to people's homes or places of work.[6] But today, not only have the channels of communication massively increased to include things like mobile phone apps and ads, social networking profiles, and viral videos, but so have the methods and means by which market researchers can understand public opinion, from online surveys to the analysis of big data.[7] Ipsos MORI stressed that this required drawing on a wide variety of skills and knowledge from social science,

'There is a science to asking questions, there is a science to data, and we can be scientific in understanding humanity and in history. There are facts. But, what is increasingly clear is that multidisciplinary teams are more productive and innovative. We need great psychologists, behavioural scientists, anthropologists, semioticians, people who deal with data, ethnographers, even documentary filmmakers. All of those things matter together. Because for us, to do social science well these days using mass data, you also need to have technical capacity and the ability to tell stories from the data. Ultimately, you need a mixture of social science, STEM and the arts and humanities.'

'The market research profession has diversified so much, and so we have had to diversify our skills and the depth and breadth of our perspectives need to be more diverse as well. So we need to hire people like anthropologists, semioticians, ethnographers, behavioural scientists, political scientists, econometricians, cultural analysts, and neuroscientists.'

STEM, and arts and humanities disciplines. For example, in order to understand the rise of a disrupter like Fortnite to the media and entertainment industries, Ipsos MORI used cultural analysts and semioticians to undertake a social science and humanities-based **analysis** of a highly technical and technological platform.[8]

Indeed, there are many parts of the Ipsos MORI business where the social sciences work in combination with other disciplines to support business functions. Within the marketing and communications division that promotes Ipsos MORI's research and thought leadership, for example, there is a **social intelligence team** that looks at data from across social media to understand today's trends. The social intelligence team aims to identify new and large trends, such as the rise of veganism, and

'How can we get social media data to help manage complaints to government, reactions to how certain policies are implemented, or reactions to certain policies themselves? Social media tracking programs can be used to understand many different things, and teams like this can train people internally in other parts of the business to use them.'

what they might mean for markets and individual behaviours that could be critically important for the company's clients, like consumer goods manufacturers. The team is made up of a small group of mixed social research specialists together with others from an information technology (IT) background. They might, for example, build tools to scan the internet to bring back social media insights to spot trends, seek early understanding of innovations, or even help understand how to manage crises.

Other examples abound, whether it is bringing together graphic designers, political scientists, and mathematicians to create impactful data

> *'The curation team unpicks existing knowledge and unlocks the value of it. It uses things like video, podcasts and immersive experiences to bring research to life and embed it with key stakeholders and audiences. Data is still the primary starting point, but the journey has to follow through to insight and become sticky with the audience... that is where the true magic lies.'*

visualisation, or using cultural analysts to understand **communities** in order to help clients with product testing or to identify unmet consumer needs. Ipsos MORI has a '**curation team**', where social science and topic experts work together with semioticians, data scientists, storytellers, and designers to 'turn multiple data sources into compelling, actionable, in-context insights'. Ipsos UU's qualitative research offerings also include its **Ethnography Centre of Excellence**, whose 'award-winning team of anthropologists, ethnographers, sociologists, film-makers, and market researchers' work together to offer their clients 'a deep understanding of consumers, helping to uncover opportunities and barriers within their associated habits, cultures, and practices'.

Social Scientists on Staff

- Sociologists	- Social policy experts
- Economists	- Human resource experts
- Behavioral economists	- Management experts
- Social researchers	- Business studies experts
- Psychologists	- Marketing experts
- Geographers	- Ethnographers
- Political scientists	- Anthropologists
- Political pollsters	- And more ...

Social scientists on staff

Not surprisingly, Ipsos MORI has a large number of social scientists on its staff from a diverse range of disciplines. Across the company, each of the different special services teams will hire

> *'We are a research business run by people who are social scientists, many of whom are incredibly technically astute. It is one of the few businesses run by 'technical' social science. That is unique to the business.'*

their own specialists, whether they are political scientists, sociologists, social and public policy experts, experts in survey methods, experts in social data analysis, anthropologists, ethnographers, or business development or strategy experts. The **Social Research Institute** in the public affairs division, for example, is one of the larger multidisciplinary teams of social scientists from sociology, economics, social research, psychology, geography, and political science and polling, and other disciplines. Many parts of the business also hire those with social science backgrounds, simply because their skills lend themselves to the work. Marketing and communications has graduates from marketing working side by side with experts in communications and graphic design, for example, but it also includes employees from a range of degrees, including economics and political science. Similarly, the human resources department has human resources management experts and psychologists (for example, working on learning and talent development), along with those with backgrounds in other social sciences. In fact, every one of the people interviewed across the upper management of Ipsos MORI highlighted that the natural curiosity of social science graduates was a key and valuable attribute they looked for when recruiting.

> *'The ability to be curious, to bring things together into a story, and to understand people – these are skills that make you successful in market research and are skills that social science graduates tend to have. And as market research becomes broader and deeper, we also need social scientists with technical skills in the industry.'*

Social impact

Market research companies like Ipsos MORI help companies to understand their consumers. They also have a role in helping governments and public sector bodies to understand their citizens and communities, and to deliver policies in a more effective way. Ipsos MORI's **Global Trends and Futures team**, for example, undertakes an annual survey asking 400 questions of 33,000 people across 33 countries to track the wider values and trends in society. The company also works with academia to conduct social science research, like its recent **collaboration** with King's College London to understand public beliefs, felt experience and behaviour under lockdown during the COVID-19 pandemic. This type of research can offer important insights for policy-makers and employers trying to deal with the crisis.

The largest area of Ipsos MORI's work is for government and the public sector. An example of this has been its work with Public Health England to increase the take up of their programmes and initiatives to improve the nation's health. Conducting a survey (online and in the field) of a representative sample of a thousand people in the UK (of different ages, gender, and working status), the resulting analysis and insights were able to help PHE better understand public awareness and perception of obesity and their programmes to reduce calorie and sugar intake. This allowed PHE to target the interventions more likely to be acceptable to the UK public, such as lowering the cost of healthier options below that of less healthy ones, and to know which interventions are less likely to be acceptable to the public, such as reducing portion sizes.[9] Ipsos MORI also helped PHE to reduce sugar consumption in children by a third through the Change 4 Life campaign, which was informed by qualitative research on perceptions and culture around sugar consumption in the UK. The 'tone in the translation of the message and relevance to the audience are the magic ingredients in driving behaviour change' such as this.[10]

'We anticipate a significant amount of the business will be automated in the future, but we don't necessarily see that as a problem for what we do, nor do we see that as a problem for social scientists. Because in the medium and long term, the need to understand why people do things will remain – as will the need to sense-check things and to validate them. These needs will persist in the public and private sphere – and increasingly understanding the public sphere is more important than it has been for a very long time.'

Looking forward

When we asked each of our Ipsos MORI interviewees

> *'We are hoping AI will develop in such a way that it will take out the routine mundane tasks that we need people to do, but which was a waste of their skills, and that it will free them up to do other things. That it will allow us to properly use the skills of the humans and the experts to look at the stories, to do the insight and analysis, and to make the judgement on the patterns that they see that look right or wrong from their experience.'*

about the future of their business, and the role of social science within it, each one believed that basic social research functions can, would and should be automated – such as the basic gathering of social data – through the use of artificial intelligence (AI). Even now, 50% of the positions within Ipsos MORI are not research roles *per se*, but roles ranging from data scientists to project managers. Yet, each person we spoke to also believed that this would lead to an even greater role for social science and social scientists in the future, as they will be needed even more to properly sift, interpret, analyse, and understand the true meaning of that data.

In the future, this will require even greater multidisciplinary working to understand people's behaviours, values, wants, and needs. One of the key issues for the future of market research, raised by a number of those that we spoke to within the company, is the need to reach younger generations, who have been raised with, and interact with, technology in a different way than older

> *'If we don't have more social scientists, if we don't have greater diversity, if we don't have more involvement, there will come a period of time where we don't have a viable business. We need to change to acknowledge that social science isn't some kind of fluffy 1970s neoliberal-type wishy-washy thing, but that it is actually an important part of who we are and what we want to offer as a business.'*

generations, but who are also more difficult to engage, in order to measure their values and opinions in a meaningful way. The consensus was that in the future the business will need a much greater range of people, skills and knowledge, in order to best engage with and understand the diversity of human behaviour, and – ultimately – the consequences for its clients from the public to the private sector.

> *'We will need more data scientists, which is a skill in its own right. And we need people who can then interpret that data and tell us what it means. We will need to have more people who are social scientists, but we don't necessarily need to badge them as quanties or qualies, and it is no longer enough to come to the table with a specific approach from one discipline. That is not enough any more. We all need to acknowledge that we will need a broader skill set.'*

Notes

1 See: https://www.ipsos.com/sites/default/files/2019-04/Ipsos-Reference-Document-2018.pdf; https://www.ipsos.com/sites/default/files/2019-04/ipsos-mori-gender-pay-gap-report-2018.pdf.

2 https://www.researchworld.com/esomars-top-20-global-companies/.

3 https://www.ipsos.com/ipsos-mori/en-uk/key-figures.

4 Bureau van Dijk (2020, April 20) Ipsos Mori UK Limited company report: Industries & Activities and Accounting Information. BvD ID no. FR304555634. Retrieved from https://orbis.bvdep.com.

5 https://www.ipsos.com/sites/default/files/2019-06/ipsos_reference_document_2018_0.pdf; https://www.ipsos.com/ipsos-mori/en-uk/solutions/list.

6 Ben Page, 'Then, Now, Next … Ipsos' 40th Anniversary,' Slide 36. https://www.slideshare.net/IpsosMORI/then-now-next-ipsos-40th-anniversary/36.

7 Ben Page, 'Then, Now, Next … Ipsos' 40th Anniversary,' Slide 36. https://www.slideshare.net/IpsosMORI/then-now-next-ipsos-40th-anniversary/36.

8 Ipsos MORI. Fortnite: Shaking the media and entertainment industry. https://www.ipsos.com/sites/default/files/ct/publication/documents/2019-04/ipsos_mori_fortnite_shaking_the_media_and_entertainment_industry_0.pdf.

9 https://www.ipsos.com/sites/default/files/ct/publication/documents/2019-02/ipsos_mori_phe_calorie_reduction_summary_public_v5.pdf.

10 https://www.ipsos.com/sites/default/files/ct/publication/documents/2018-06/the_power_of_culture_final.pdf.

Company: Royal Dutch Shell

Industry: Energy **Website: Shell.com**
Size: Large MNC **HQ: The Hague, The Netherlands**

- As with all the other businesses, social sciences are used in the day-to-day and long-term running of the business (for instance, through management, business, law, finance, economics, etc.)
- Social sciences such as politics and geography are used in country-specific research, planning, and risk-management
- Social sciences are used in scenario-planning to take account of possible future developments in, for instance, regulation, digitalisation, and energy use

Royal Dutch Shell plc ('Shell') is a large multinational energy company incorporated in England and Wales and headquartered in the Netherlands. In 2019, it had a revenue of $345 billion (USD) and around 83,000 employees globally.[1] Its business lines can be divided into *Upstream* business (covering activities including exploration for and production of oil and gas); *Integrated Gas and New Energies* business (covering activities from producing and transporting liquified natural gas to renewables such as wind and solar); *Downstream* business (covering activities from the production, trading, and selling of oil products and chemicals); and *Projects and Technology* business (covering activities from the delivery of major projects to research and development). These businesses are supported by Shell's *Corporate* division which covers their holdings and treasury organisation, self-insurance activities, headquarters and central functions.[2] Across these reporting lines, Shell undertakes various business activities which can be grouped under the headings of: exploration; development and extraction; manufacturing and energy production; transport and trading; sales and marketing; and technical and business services.[3] Some of these will occur across multiple areas of the business, such as marketing (a social science discipline), which will have teams in the Upstream, Downstream, and the Integrated Gas and New

Energies business lines. This case study will look across the company and focus in on work done by some of the specific teams within Shell.

Social sciences at work

Like most large companies in any industry, Shell requires input from a wide variety of social science disciplines. This includes advice from legal professionals to understand the legal implications and regulatory risks of its activities, as well as knowledge from business studies to develop the company's portfolio and strategy. Shell also draws on knowledge from the discipline of finance to fund its many projects and grow its portfolio, and also for the knowledge of trading that it uses across its business to trade oil, gas, and power. The company uses

'Business management and leadership require an understanding of the social sciences. That is a very broad term, but if anyone is pursuing a career where they need to work with other people, lead other people, manage other people on a daily basis, or manage their work – it is difficult to imagine that they could just operate and be distant from the social sciences. In general, business management requires engagement with the social sciences. Of course, the human resources functions, marketing, strategy, industrial relations, and investor relations ... all need to understand the social sciences, and how the image of the organisation is created and communicated through some of the social science principles.'

'Even those in the technical careers and technical sciences, very often get engaged with some additional development (whether leadership development or further education) to develop their understanding of human behaviour and organisational behaviour and business sciences.'

accounting for the daily running of its business and reporting to investors. Its External Relations and Investor Relations functions draw on knowledge from many social science disciplines, from communications, to accounting, to political science to communicate Shell's activities effectively to a variety of stakeholders. Social science evidence related to marketing is also critical across Shell's business lines and while much of this is done in the Downstream areas of the business (for example marketing to individuals and industrial companies), Shell's Upstream business must also market its activities and products to governments, which is a very different process of engagement. Management studies are also vital – from managing the daily workings of a large company including human resources management, to supply chain, organisational, and logistics management. Those in management and leadership positions, even in the technical and engineering side of the business, will normally hold at least some sort of higher degree or pursue further learning in social sciences, such as master's degrees in business administration or management studies, or courses in leadership.

'Organisational identity is really the interplay between the organisational culture and the external perceptions of the organisation. How do we use social science in shaping this at Shell? Well, we base our approach on certain social theories ... we look at a particular challenge the business is grappling with, what the question is that we are trying to answer, and then look at the latest thinking in the field ... usually looking at social psychology, anthropological, and psychological theories that may help us frame the question we are working with, and provide us with a lens to understand it. Our research looks at social theories and their core concepts — and we reach out and explore those concepts with academics in the field, to shape our approach based on our informed views through social theories.'

Another example of the use of the social sciences at Shell is in the area of *organisational development and learning*. At Shell, this team focuses on organisational change, helping the company evolve its identity and culture, working with senior leaders in the business to support them through leading and shaping sustainable change. This can, for example, include leadership development and coaching at the individual, team and organisational levels, especially for teams and individuals who might be underperforming, have new joiners, need to reshape their purpose or role, who are from different cultures, or are geographically dispersed and need to foster a sense of belonging. The organisational development team also works on the organisational structures and operational models of the company, on cultural change within the company, and on changes to HR policies and processes, such as how they recruit, identify and attract talent or promote talent within the organisation.

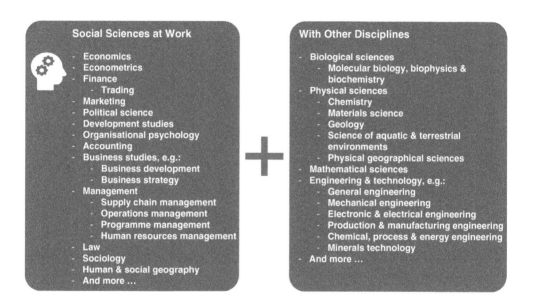

Social sciences working with other sciences

Shell also has numerous multidisciplinary teams and lines of business that draw on the social sciences. Its *country review* work, for example, monitors and reviews the situation in the different countries where the company is engaged. They look at issues like the political stability and accessibility in a particular country, how it is changing, what that depends on, and the political, regulatory, legal, and security risks implied. Knowledge of political science, sociology, development studies, economics, and law are all important for such work. This research is used internally, but also shared, for example with governments that the company works with on a regular basis. The company will also sometimes review energy systems in different countries and discuss these with relevant governments

'Our research work for the scenarios, like that in our country reviews or global scenarios, needs to stay detached from what the rest of the business is trying to do. Scenarios are there to test the business, not to be a marketing arm for it. So we need to balance working with the businesses in Shell, from a certain detachment. The Shell scenarios have a long-standing reputation for independence and it's important for our credibility and usefulness that we maintain that. Unlike the Shell businesses, we are not looking to go out with particular products or services to appeal to customers.'

to help build a better understanding of possible changes in national energy supplies. This work often draws on both social science disciplines and STEM disciplines.

An excellent example of a multidisciplinary research team within Shell is its _scenarios team_, which produces long-term scenarios, or 'alternate futures'. These include scenarios for the global energy system. The team itself is multidisciplinary, made up of economists, political scientists, engineers, mathematicians, and environmental scientists (to name but a few) and takes an explicitly multidisciplinary approach. This is because of their need to take into account a wide range of factors both within and outside the energy market, including economic, geographic, geological, scientific, technological, social, and political factors. The team draws on social science and STEM knowledge from both within the team and from external experts to ensure that they are considering a wide range of possible pathways for the future.

'There is often a tendency in the modelling community to focus only on the technology and the economic cost of things, but when one actually looks at the evidence we see that so many energy decisions have actually revolved around other factors. Our team has a multidisciplinary philosophy because just looking at the energy markets won't tell you the whole story, and you might be blind-sided if you miss an important factor from another domain.'

This work can include, for example, economics-based statistical models of how energy prices are changing, how economies are changing and how energy use is changing. Political science is important for understanding the future possibilities within national (and global) energy systems, as politics is crucial to many national energy decisions and energy security is a key concern for many countries. The team also needs to take into consideration things like legal and regulatory risk, which play a large role in scenario planning. For factors like demography and human and social geography,

> 'Energy security is seen as a national priority by many countries. What resources you have in your country, or which countries you are reliant on for your energy imports (or who you might export to if you have energy surpluses in your country), has been something that countries take seriously – so politics does matter. And there has been a discussion about, again with energy transitions, what all of this is likely to mean for changes in the strategic political power points in the world.'

> 'Part of our ethos is that we can't possibly internally reflect the expertise that a whole university department would have, let alone a wider discipline in a particular area. What we can try to do is to have people with expertise in these different areas to draw on, and distil that down so that we can try to join the dots. The silo-based way of the academic world can sometimes be missing this multidisciplinary element. In the scenarios team we try to get people with different perspectives, so that we can try to flesh these things out together.'

they will often bring in expertise from outside the company and have, for example, often worked with universities.

Indeed, Shell has established relationships with various bodies, institutions and professional organisations to engage knowledge from the social science and STEM disciplines, and different teams in the company will often participate in and collaborate with academic experts. The scenarios team, for example, has links with MIT, Imperial, UCL, and Cambridge University, as well as with specific individuals who are recognised names within their fields. For example, Shell is a sponsor of the MIT Global Change program that is looking to model global change, taking into account different environmental, economic, and political scenarios.

Understanding issues like land use or bioenergy, for example, cannot be done without a multidisciplinary approach that includes both the technical and social sciences. In another example, even understanding how digitalisation can affect energy use benefitted from having external experts from a range of social science as well as STEM disciplines to consider different scenarios related to privacy, centralised digital systems or the rise in the use of autonomous vehicles, and the resulting implications for energy needs and consumption.

There are, of course, many other multidisciplinary teams across Shell tackling important issues. For example, the *group portfolio* team looks at the group's strategy in the long term, considering important issues like resilience that must be taken into consideration for the Shell portfolio – whether that is financial or economic resilience, the risk profile of different projects, or their geographic spread.

Social Scientists on Staff

- Architects
- Landscape architects
- Planners (urban, rural and regional)
- Human & social geographers
- Economists
- Management experts
  - Human resources management experts
- Business experts
- Finance & accounting experts
- Marketing experts
- Sociologists
- Public policy experts
- Social policy experts
- Development studies experts
- Lawyers
- And more ...

Social scientists on staff

There are a wide range of social scientists and those with social science backgrounds working at Shell. In marketing, legal, finance and trading, accounting, and human resources teams, for example, there are many with specialist social science degrees in their fields. The organisational learning and development team includes staff with master's degrees and PhDs in psychology and organisational psychology. In areas like branding, marketing, communications (internal and external), and sales there will be a range of professionals with different social science backgrounds from psychology to business studies. There are a number of other teams with high numbers of social scientists as well, such as the Energy Transitions Program and the Net Carbon Footprint Initiative, which explore how Shell can lower the carbon intensity of the energy it uses and provides. As with the scenarios team, these teams often work in collaboration with other partners in a range of sectors.

If we again take the Shell scenarios team as an example, it includes about 20 people in the global team, with two-thirds in the Netherlands and one-third in the UK. A small portion of the team have a mathematics background, but most come to

'The 3 main pillars of our scenarios work are politics, economics and energy analysis. In energy there is a mixture of us, but more of the people are more engineering orientated.'

the team with either business or engineering backgrounds. There are also several political analysts with specific political science training and higher degrees, and some economists with higher degrees in economics.

'Very often social science graduates have a curiosity and ability to relate to their colleagues, and the interpersonal skills and capabilities to understand the dynamics in working with other people. That is helpful. Understanding the psychology of individuals, teams, and groups – that helps them perform their jobs. Those with higher degrees in the social sciences have a clear understanding of research – how to evaluate, interpret, and read research that uses different methodologies, recognise its significance or limitations – that they can apply beyond their own fields. The social sciences equip people with these transferable skills that they can apply in other contexts.'

Employees with social science backgrounds and degrees are valued across the company for their understanding of how social systems and organisations work, as well as for their other capabilities.

Social impact

During the current COVID-19 pandemic, in addition to putting in safeguards for a very large workforce needed to keep the company's energy supply chains moving, Shell has also diverted a portion of its chemical operations to make increased amounts of isopropyl alcohol (IPA), which is used as a base for hand sanitiser. Shell is making available 2.5 million litres of IPA to the Dutch healthcare sector and donating 125,000 litres of IPA to the government of Canada. They are also supporting in other ways, for example offering free fuel to healthcare providers and ambulances in countries including Brunei, Bulgaria, Mexico, the Netherlands, Oman, Poland, Russia and Turkey.[4]

Environmental change is another issue that requires a multidisciplinary approach. It is important that energy companies like Shell work with governments, other industry leaders, stakeholders, and society to ensure that they are operating in a safe, positive, and environmentally responsible way, to provide 'oil, gas and low-carbon energy as the world's energy system transforms'.[5] Shell has committed itself to making the business sustainable by providing 'more and cleaner energy solutions in a responsible way' in the context of a world that will likely have a third higher population, and a third more energy demand, by 2050.[6] To this end, for example, Shell has set itself an ambition to become, by 2050 or sooner, a net-zero emissions energy business.[7]

Looking forward

In terms of the future of work at Shell, there is a clear recognition that good social science skills will need to be combined with good technical

> '*A lot of repetitive tasks can be automated, but what cannot be automated are human relations – the interactions and relationships between the people who need to get the work done. Increasingly, we are blending the technology and science with good organisational management and psychological processes to improve how teams work together. This interaction between the social sciences and technology will be required, and valued as essential, for the business in the future.*'

science skills to develop the energy system of the future. There is a clear recognition among those we talked to that the future will be a much more interdisciplinary environment where social, physical, and technical scientists will all need to work together to tackle real business and societal issues like those posed by climate change.

> '*It is an interesting question to think 'how might the energy system change in the future?' Will people, for example, want more managed outdoor environments, like stadiums being air conditioned in preparation for the Qatar World Cup? The futurists can run wild with these things, so we have to be careful to stay grounded and not devolve into science fiction. So there has been an increasing realisation in the modelling community that you really need to understand the social and human behaviour aspect of all of this. We can't just think about energy as doing other or new things. We need to look at the practices people are involved in, and at how are those changing to influence energy, rather than the other way around.*'

Notes

1   https://reports.shell.com/annual-report/2019/.
2   https://reports.shell.com/annual-report/2019/strategic-report/strategy-business-and-market-overview/our-business-model-explained.php.

3   https://reports.shell.com/annual-report/2019/strategic-report/strategy-business-and-market-overview/our-business-model-explained.php.

4   https://www.shell.com/covid19/covid-19-shells-global-response.html.

5   https://www.shell.com/about-us/what-we-do.html.

6   https://www.shell.com/energy-and-innovation/the-energy-future/what-is-shells-net-carbon-footprint-ambition.html.

7   https://www.shell.com/energy-and-innovation/the-energy-future/shells-ambition-to-be-a-net-zero-emissions-energy-business.html.

Company: Willis Towers Watson

Industry: Reinsurance Brokerage Services

Size: Large Enterprise

Website: www.willistowerswatson.com

HQ: Dublin, Ireland

- Social sciences are used in many projects related to climate change – this is often about managing risk, changing people's behaviours and perceptions, and understanding the local and demographic factors that may affect these
- Social sciences are also used in other projects, from those involving the 'transition risks' around the medium to long-term social, political and behavioural changes that can affect reinsurance, to those looking at the spatial diversification of risk
- Social scientists from external academic departments are sometimes involved to help ensure wide exposure to a range of expertise and views

Willis Towers Watson is a global advisory, broking and solutions business with a focus on helping clients to manage risk in times and contexts of uncertainty. It has around 45,000 employees serving over 140 countries and markets, with a turnover of over £6.5 billion in 2018. Willis Towers Watson's principal service lines are: (1) Human Capital and Benefits (HCB), which provides advice and services to management, human resources, and benefits teams; (2) Corporate Risk and Broking (CRB), which offers insurance broking, consulting, and risk advice to a broad range of industries in the financial, property, and transport sectors; (3) Investment,

> 'Insurance needs a social licence to operate and it is also a fundamentally social activity. There is a cultural relationship between the public and the private sector when negotiating who carries the risk from natural disasters, for example. And as part of that process there are many social science components that people might not quite expect, if they are only looking at things at a superficial level.'

Risk, and Reinsurance (IRR), which offers consulting and services to manage risk, insurance, and investment through, for example, the provision of 'reserves opinions, software, ratemaking, risk underwriting, and reinsurance broking'; and finally, (4) Benefits Delivery and Administration (BDA), which 'provides primary medical and ancillary benefit exchange and outsourcing services to active employees and retirees across both the group and individual markets'.[1]

This case study focuses largely on the risk and reinsurance side of the business (CRB and IRR), and particularly the Climate and Resilience Hub, which has a strong applied research component in its focus on emerging risks, disaster risk financing and innovative solutions.

Social sciences at work

The social sciences play a critical role in Willis Towers Watson's work. Across the larger business, there is naturally the need to draw on business and management research – especially human resource management, economics, and the study of finance and financial products – as well as disciplinary expertise from geography and political science. A key business task is risk assessment, where a prime focus is on the impact of natural hazards (wind, floods, earthquakes, tsunamis, etc.) on humans, biodiversity, and the built environment. To understand the impacts of these natural hazards, they need to draw on knowledge from political science to understand the political risk, on human and social geography to understand the geographic and demographic risk factors – even aspects of urbanisation and where people live are important.

'When one considers the ESG factors as they are called – Environment, Social and Governance factors – around investment, that always includes a considerable social sciences component of understanding the impacts of potential investments and how attractive that is to people, as we are aware more and more of shareholder action, for example, and investor sentiment, and want to know how companies invest and what they invest in, and what the impact of that work is.'

One key component of the business is understanding the 'transition risk' that may arise when a business is disrupted by physical events (like climate events), or by social, behavioural, and technological changes, such as the shift to electric vehicles or changes in energy supply, that will affect market opportunities in 5 or 10 years. In order to help companies, Willis Towers Watson can build models for forecasting such transitions; to do so they need to consider population, demographic, economic, and key behavioural changes that accompany them.

This also requires understanding who is buying these insurance products, and what type of products they may want to consume in 5 or 10 years – and understanding the impact that generational and other socio-cultural changes will have on how valuable those products will be in the future. This more broadly based sectoral research could be an example of the broader 'R&D' work that is not well captured in official statistics.

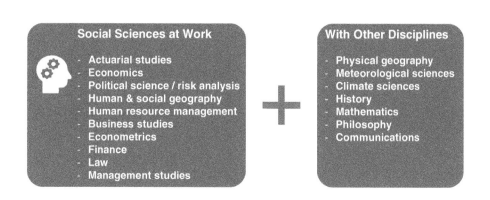

Social Sciences at Work
- Actuarial studies
- Economics
- Political science / risk analysis
- Human & social geography
- Human resource management
- Business studies
- Econometrics
- Finance
- Law
- Management studies

With Other Disciplines
- Physical geography
- Meteorological sciences
- Climate sciences
- History
- Mathematics
- Philosophy
- Communications

Social sciences working with other sciences

Willis Towers Watson has studied physical climate risk, like floods and storms, for over 30 years, and draws heavily on disciplinary knowledge from physical geography, meteorology, and other physical sciences. There is also a fair amount of mathematical modelling involved in the firm's work, some of which draws from the quantitative social sciences methods (like econometrics and financial modelling), some from the physical sciences (like physical hazard modelling) and some from the mathematical sciences. But in order to get a full picture of, for example, climate risk, risk assessment teams need to be multidisciplinary in the knowledge they draw from, and to be multimethod in terms of the skills that they apply in order to be able to paint a comprehensive and understandable picture for their clients.

On the broader spectrum of risks, Willis Towers Watson also looks into issues like drought and pandemic that require interdisciplinary approaches. The firm worked with the World Bank, for example, during the Ebola outbreak on 'catastrophe bonds' for pandemics. In that case, anthropologists played an important role in understanding the risks with respect to burial ceremonies and the effect that had on the spread of the disease. The Climate and Resilience Hub also needed broad disciplinary collaboration to create insurance products for issues such as coral reef conservation in the context of environmental change. The increased potential for storms with global warming can affect coastal ecosystems that bring in important income for local populations from both fishing and tourism, and insurance products covering such ecosystems can help build in resilience for these communities.[2] The Willis Research Network (WRN) has, therefore, partnered with a multidisciplinary team at the University of Exeter, which includes social environmental scientists and geographers, working together with members of the biological, life, meteorological, and aquaculture sciences.[3]

In order to get a good mix of knowledge from a wide range of disciplines and fields, the whole Willis Towers Watson firm has access to the WRN,

> '*I am employed to be a quantifier and I appreciate that there is an aspect of having to strip away and communicate via numbers because that allows markets to compare and trade internationally. But numbers never speak for themselves, so we are always going back to that narrative social component. I am delighted when I work with NGOs and IOs that increasingly have more numerate personnel, and that is very useful for me. But I appreciate the value that comes from the social sciences, whether that is economics or psychology, which all play into aspects of our work.*'

> *'I have found both the physical and human components of geography extremely useful to be able to talk to lots of clients, and I have always been happy to work in the interface between business, applied research, and academia.'*

which for over 10 years now has been building relationships with academic institutions internationally. Much of this work is built around STEM activities and disciplines with respect to understanding particular aspects of natural hazards (tropical cyclones, atmospheric physics, building responses to pressure waves, etc.), but the WRN has also worked with social science departments at various universities to better understand the type of impacts these hazards cause and to better understand some transition risks, as discussed above. The WRN, for example, is also

> *'Education is inevitably more specialised in the UK at an earlier age, and that is a shame because many lose the ability to communicate across disciplines early on. Specialist experts are required, particularly for regulatory requirements. However, for innovation, the most fertile ground – for building new products and applying research – is in the overlap between disciplines.'*

currently working with a social science department at the University of Loughborough to better understand how artificial intelligence will affect society and the insurance industry.[4] In addition to reaching out to academia, Willis Towers Watson also has forums with other companies, and put together roundtables and workshops on particular issues of interest.

Social scientists on staff

Willis Towers Watson has a wide range of graduate and postgraduate employment across the disciplines.

The human capital and benefits departments, for example, have a large number of people with social science backgrounds, who can provide internal expertise on issues like the impact of the fourth industrial revolution

> '*Insurance and reinsurance are relationship businesses. It is about negotiating and relationships. There is a STEM component of quantifying risk, but equally that quantified risk sits inside a broader narrative of risk communication, which is a deeply human activity, and which requires a certain amount of breadth that you don't necessarily get from maths graduates alone. Within the mix of skills and personality types that are valuable for team diversity, ideally you need a few 'renaissance people' that can cross these boundaries. This requires graduates with breadth. More and more I see that aspect of the social sciences in our work, and in the fundamental foundations of the institutions that we work in.*'

for clients and the business itself. There are a variety of research teams. The investment business, for example, has a **thinking ahead institute**, whose team includes those with degrees ranging from applied statistics and physics in STEM, to actuarial, finance, business, and economics in the social sciences.

Willis Towers Watson is the world's biggest private sector employer of actuaries – which is a social science combining high-level mathematics with a 'unique combination of analytical and business skills' to address and help find solutions to a wide range of both 'financial and social problems'.[5] The insurance industry is also a major employer of geographers – both physical, and human and social geographers – because the fundamental principle of insurance is the diversification of risk, which inevitably has a spatial component. Lawyers, including those with international expertise, are also crucial when, for example, the company is working with the World Bank and the UN to construct insurance products for developing economies, including the role that insurance might play in supporting humanitarian aid.

Substantive knowledge gained at degree level can also be important. Psychology is an obvious example for an

> '*There is usually a baseline level where you can find lots of people with the technical skills you are after, and then it is the question of what distinguishes candidates on top of that*'

insurance company, because those in a broking role must be able to use negotiation and the understanding of relationships and human behaviour to convince underwriters to give them a good deal and the best price for their clients. Economists are also needed for their substantive economic understanding as well their methodological skills.

If we look, for example, at the Graduate Development Program (GDP) intake across part, but not all of Willis Towers Watson, including Willis Re (reinsurance broking) and Corporate Risk and Broking (CRB), 69% of the 71 people hired from 2016 to 2019 have social science degrees, with little variation year on year (see graph below). In reality, this number might be slightly lower, as a portion of the geographers hired may be physical geographers rather than human and social geographers. Interestingly, the discipline with the largest numbers hired is economics (at more than 18%), with 'geography' (at more than 11%), business studies (at 7%), and politics (at almost 6%).[6]

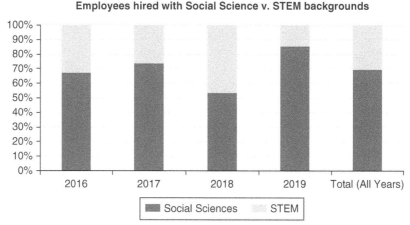

Social impact

The provision of advice, insurance, reinsurance, and risk assessment helps those in the private and public sector to navigate uncertainty and to mitigate the negative effects of catastrophic events. Whether it is events that are increasingly common in the context of climate change, like tsunamis, or

'When you are working with local governments and companies, they like to see that you are engaged with local research institutions, because it builds trust and shows opportunities for both tech transfer and capacity building and, effectively, the products that you build will be more robust and successful for it.'

historic challenges, like piracy, risk and (re)insurance services help dampen the negative consequences and provide relief that allows societies and companies to rebuild. Clients in such cases include insurance and reinsurance companies and other corporates, as well as cities, governments, non-governmental organisations and inter-governmental organisations, For example, financial products are developed for emerging market countries to protect their economies, lives, and livelihoods against the ravages of natural hazards and some aspects of climate change.

Much of Willis Towers Watson's work considers the role insurance and risk management processes may play in developing societal resilience. This includes, for example, work with governments and UN agencies. Recently, Willis Towers Watson set up the Insurance Development Forum, bringing together private sector, public sector, and other stakeholder organisations to look at what is known as the 'protection gap' – the many people without any form of social protection against the impact of natural hazards, like floods, droughts, and food issues, and related political risk. For practical reasons, a key aspect of all of this work is in-country knowledge and engagement – in addition to remote sensing data sets, and access to leading international academic institutions, local knowledge is crucial. That knowledge can take many forms: it might be knowledge of where data exists, but also crucially how to interpret that data in the light of understanding the political and social conditions in a country. The social sciences can also help assess the success of projects, very often involving donor aid money, to provide valuable feedback about how well policies are working to foster social resilience. The Climate and Resilience Hub often tries to work alongside NGOs (such as Save the Children, and the Start Network), the Overseas Development Institute, and various other international development agencies, and local teams, either to assist with action aid, for example, or to look at aspects of environmental and social justice.

Looking forward

Society, particularly the industrialised West, will be going through dramatic changes in the next 30 years, due to climatic pressures, regulatory changes, the increasing impact of big data and new bio-technologies – to name but a few. In order to be agile enough to

'One can get patterns from data, and machine learning can show us statistical relationships, but then you need to be able to explain them and sort the wheat from the chaff – and that is where that interpretation component of the social sciences comes in.'

understand and respond to these changes, businesses like Willis Towers Watson need flexibility of outlook and the greater ability to work across disciplines with diverse teams drawing on different knowledge pools and skill sets. Insurance and reinsurance companies, like Willis Towers Watson, need to understand, for example, how changes like the adoption of autonomous vehicles or the shift to renewable energy will change risk profiles for companies and revolutionise automotive and other forms of insurance products. Similarly, there are pressing questions about how to provide financial and insurance products for new working practices and business structures, which means that there is a role increasingly for the social sciences in the financial sector as it seeks to better understand the interactions between human behaviour and finance.

Notes

1   https://investors.willistowerswatson.com/static-files/a6ef28ea-6203-47f0-9c22-8040f61cfaf0.
2   https://www.willistowerswatson.com/en-GB/Insights/2018/07/what-impact-could-changing-storminess-have-on-global-fisheries.
3   https://www.nature.com/articles/s41558-018-0206-x.
4   https://www.willistowerswatson.com/en-GB/Insights/2019/11/artificial-intelligence-ai-and-emerging-business-models-in-insurance.
5   psuactsci.com/what-is-an-actuary.html.
6   Numbers estimated by interviewee at Willis Towers Watson, with the assistance of their human resources department.

Company: WSP

Industry: Business Services
        (Engineering Consulting)
Size: Large MNC

Website: www.wsp.com

HQ: Montreal, Canada

- Social sciences, including planning and geography, are often used in understanding regional and local issues and contexts
- Social sciences are also used in larger spatial studies on projects of national importance
- Social sciences are used in designing and working on appropriate consultations and effective collaborations with affected communities

WSP provides engineering and technical consulting and professional services for projects of all shapes and sizes across the globe. Headquartered in Canada, the parent firm employed 48,000 people worldwide and had a turnover of £5.8b in 2018. This case study focuses on WSP's UK subsidiary, which employed 6,676 people and had a turnover of $862m that same year. WSP UK Ltd provides management and consultancy services for 'aspects of the built and natural environment, ranging from management, engineering, and planning to environmental advice',[1] and is one of the UK's major multidisciplinary consultancies, with clients in both public and private sectors.[2] The company operates through four strategic business units in the UK: (1) Transport & Infrastructure; (2) Planning & Advisory; (3) Property & Buildings; and (4) Energy & Industry. In the UK, WSP works in over 40 economic sectors (from aviation and tunnelling, to pharma and biotech)[3] and provides over 140 discrete types of services, from bridge design and coastal engineering, to project and stakeholder management.[4]

Social sciences at work with other disciplines

Each of the work streams in WSP UK draw on the social sciences in some way. First, they are all supported by the social sciences fundamental to the running of any business – such as legal, business, management, human resources, finance, accounting, and marketing knowledge and skills.

Multidisciplinary working is also typical of WSP's different workstreams. WSP's Transport & Logistics stream uses social science knowledge from urban,

'In the engineering space, innovative solutions are constantly evolving and being developed to prepare our world for its everyday challenges. I think that social scientists provide the interpretation of imperfect data, in a way that's different to engineers. Their strengths and weaknesses mirror our own. It is a very complementary relationship.'

– Ashley Parry Jones BA BSc CGeog FRGS
Director, Planning
Head of Profession, Land Services

rural, and regional planning, as well as expertise in business management and operations management to design and deliver projects.[5] Property & Buildings projects rely on the social sciences, as well as the technical elements of architecture, landscape architecture, and building, together with STEM disciplines like engineering. Projects in the Energy & Industry stream draw on the knowledge of planners, geographers, and experts in finance to work in concert with environmental and other scientists on issues such as sustainable water use management. WSP's Planning & Advisory business stream draws on a wide variety of social sciences, from planning and geography, business and management, finance and evaluation, to political science and social policy. Expertise in planning is essential to ensure successful completion of projects, and WSP uses multidisciplinary teams to help their clients understand the 'unique combination of demands, in a unique physical setting, under unique commercial and institutional constraints' of each project, because 'achieving a balance between performance, productivity, and cost-effectiveness requires a thorough, simultaneous examination of all issues'.[6]

'As an engineering consultancy, WSP has many projects that will be more engineering led, but social scientists play an essential role in providing challenge and ensure solutions are applicable in a real-world situation. They provide a different voice and a different way of thinking. Engineers work to establish technical standards. Whereas social scientists are optimizers – its not about perfection, but about an optimal decision that satisfies multiple parameters at once. That is a very different type of conversation, and I think that is a really useful challenge that social scientists provide.'

– Ashley Parry Jones

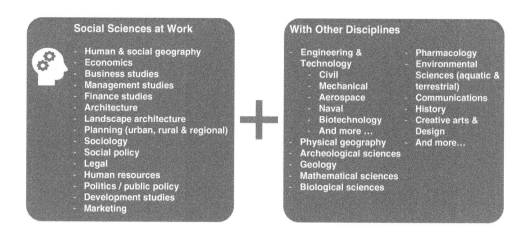

Social Sciences at Work

- Human & social geography
- Economics
- Business studies
- Management studies
- Finance studies
- Architecture
- Landscape architecture
- Planning (urban, rural & regional)
- Sociology
- Social policy
- Legal
- Human resources
- Politics / public policy
- Development studies
- Marketing

With Other Disciplines

- Engineering & Technology
  - Civil
  - Mechanical
  - Aerospace
  - Naval
  - Biotechnology
  - And more …
- Physical geography
- Archeological sciences
- Geology
- Mathematical sciences
- Biological sciences

- Pharmacology
- Environmental Sciences (aquatic & terrestrial)
- Communications
- History
- Creative arts & Design
- And more…

Social scientists on staff

WSP has on its staff architects, landscape architects, urban, regional, and rural planners, lawyers, marketing experts, accountants, human resource managers, business and management experts, economists and those with backgrounds in geography, politics, social policy, and development studies – to name but a few. A good example of how these social scientists, and employees with social science skills, work within WSP is to look at the 400-person team within Planning & Advisory that helps with planning permission for complicated infrastructure development projects, such as HS2, Crossrail and Heathrow expansion. This team is led by a geographer, as it manages large sets of spatial data, but it is heavily multidisciplinary. Some team members hail from STEM disciplines (such as engineering and the environmental sciences), while some are from the humanities (such as communications experts), and

'We interact with a lot of disciplines – some physical and technical disciplines that you would expect to find in infrastructure project planning, but also with a lot of social scientists, who are often the glue holding those more hard engineering-based disciplines together, helping them to find a context and the reasons why the engineering solutions are the right solutions. We work together and try to provide that context.'

-- Ashley Parry Jones

'It is no coincidence that WSP has a few hundred social scientists in the UK alone.'

-- Ashley Parry Jones

some are from social sciences that can provide understanding of social context, such as geographers, urban planners, public and social policy experts, or marketing experts.

Social Scientists on Staff

- Architects
- Landscape architects
- Planners (urban, rural and regional)
- Human & social geographers
- Economists
- Management experts
  - Human resources management experts
- Business experts
- Finance & accounting experts
- Marketing experts
- Sociologists
- Public policy experts
- Social policy experts
- Development studies experts
- Lawyers
- And more ...

Social impact

In its work on engineering projects in the UK, WSP values a multidisciplinary approach. This case study shows how STEM and social science disciplines can work together to ensure that large infrastructure projects conducted by WSP are environmentally positive and provide benefits to local communities.

Within WSP's Planning & Advisory stream of work, there is a stakeholder engagement and consultation team, whose employees have a range of degrees, including history, English, marketing, politics, and economics. Their work experience, combined with their disciplinary knowledge, helps stakeholders and the general public make sense of the complicated planning processes and engineering requirements of specific projects. Staff expertise includes understanding of the demographic, economic, development, and social needs of the communities who may be affected, and the skills to ensure that stakeholder surveys and consultations are representative and informative. The larger infrastructure and engineering projects that WSP works on require serious engagement with the affected communities – not only because UK laws and regulation require it, but also because this ensures projects deliver the best possible benefits to affected communities, in the long run as well as the short term.[7] This requires robust evaluation techniques of a project's impact, understanding the economics of a geographic space, grasping the local demographics that will help explain how to best achieve good outcomes, and understanding how best to communicate a project's plans.

> '*High level master planning is largely driven by economics. But there will be other projects where ... we will need to understand the demographics of that part of the world in order to best cater to, or mitigate, or best engage with those people. We have people who are there to provide some analysis of local demographics, and from that derive appropriate methodologies for engagement and try to understand what makes people tick and how we can make the experience of having development imposed as smooth as possible.*'
>
> *— Ashley Parry Jones*

Another example of the importance of social science knowledge and skills can be found in some of the recent infrastructure-led regeneration projects in London in areas like White City, King's Cross, and Wembley. A recent

> *'By using our insight as social scientists, and drawing on many of the aspects of all social sciences – geography but also business, planning, economics, sociology, landscape architecture, –*
> *we can convey really complicated information on the legal, planning, and engineering details of a project, while also engaging the people who are most affected by these proposals. We listen to them and ensure that we are reacting and helping them to make appropriate decisions about how they want to react to these proposals.'*
>
> *-- Ashley Parry Jones*

report by WSP and London First found that there were several common key ingredients for successful delivery of these types of projects – in addition to optimal use of existing transport, land, and infrastructure – including thoughtfully sequenced funding, the availability of patient capital (i.e. – capital invested for the long term), the optimal use of cultural assets through creation of a 'brand' or by building on existing architectural heritage, and having a 'collaborative relationship with [the] local borough' that entailed 'working with local leaders to build a place that enhances opportunity for local people and fits with local economic development plans'.[8] Each of these four 'key ingredients' for successful infrastructure and engineering-led development requires social science skills. Thoughtful funding and the use of patient capital require knowledge of finance, accounting, business and economics. Working with local leaders for positive collaborative development requires urban planners, those with good knowledge of public and social policy, and urban economic growth and development. And, of course, creating a brand requires solid marketing expertise.

> *'We consciously pull from a really broad array of disciplines – including the social sciences – to make sure that we are influencing the engineering design in a way which is sympathetic to the surrounding communities. Our employees work from their own experiences of doing these projects, as well as from the disciplinary knowledge that they have studied or learnt in their specialist careers.'*
>
> *-- Ashley Parry Jones*

Looking forward

> 'A lot of the projects I work on deliver infrastructure improvement but also go far beyond this to deliver on economic factors and urban regeneration. They are about using national projects to deliver local benefit.'
>
> — Ashley Parry Jones

The industry around engineering-led projects in infrastructure and the environment has changed dramatically in the UK over the last several decades. Twenty years ago, large-scale engineering projects were often viewed with suspicion and concern, in part because of the upheaval that they would cause to their neighbours. But the success of projects like the King's Cross area regeneration, which have demonstrated the positive economic and social

> 'The tools with which these complicated planning processes are conveyed, and the way that companies like WSP, their clients and communities realise benefits, are changing. And social scientists have an important role to play in that.'
>
> — Ashley Parry Jones

> 'Policy changes continue to make impacts on the built environment that require more social scientists. Policies that require consultations and that put more community engagements at the heart of planning processes, must need more social scientists. One relies on the other. I consider Britain to be a nation that builds infrastructure in a more considered way, that is looking for additional benefits, and I think we are getting much better at it.'
>
> — Ashley Parry Jones

benefits when infrastructure investment is focused and used as a conduit to larger transformation, means that social views of these projects are changing. They are now more often seen as providing opportunities for more jobs, more office space, more homes, more schools, and greater improvements to the lives of local communities. As a result, a greater number of STEM and social science disciplines are required not only to be involved in the planning, design, management and delivery of these projects, but also in putting them in a wider context, with clear social justification. Social sciences like marketing, survey research and evaluation, and social studies can be helpful. The legislation behind these projects has also changed, so that proper consultation with affected communities is required by law and must be done to a particular standard. Ensuring that communities are now front and centre in these projects requires that social science disciplines are involved in the stakeholder engagement, analysis, and delivery of the benefits that communities now expect.

Notes

1   Bureau van Dijk (2020, March 10) WSP UK Limited company report: Products and services. Retrieved from https://orbis.bvdep.com.
2   Bureau van Dijk (2020, March 10) WSP UK Limited company report: Size estimate. Retrieved from https://orbis.bvdep.com.
3   https://www.wsp.com/en-GL/sectors.
4   https://www.wsp.com/en-GL/services.
5   https://www.wsp.com/en-GL/hubs/maritime.
6   https://www.wsp.com/en-GB/hubs/planning-and-advisory.
7   https://www.wsp.com/en-GB/insights/the-future-of-social-value-in-developments.
8   WSP and London First. 'West London: Delivering the Opportunities' (29 October 2019). Available at: https://www.wsp.com/en-GB/news/2019/new-report-reviews-success-stories-west-london.